The military police photographer known as Caesar
was required to document the murder and torture of
thousands of Syrian civilians in the custody of the Assad
regime. Over the course of two years he used a police
computer to copy the photos, and in 2013 he risked his
life to smuggle out 53,000 photos and documents that
show prisoners tortured, starved and burned to death.

In January 2015, in the American magazine *Foreign
Affairs*, President Bashar al-Assad claimed that this
military photographer didn't exist. 'Who took the
pictures? Who is he? Nobody knows. There is no verification of any of this evidence, so it's all allegations
without evidence.'

Caesar exists. The author of this book has spent dozens
of hours with him. His testimony is extraordinary, his
photos shocking. The uncovering of the workings of
the Syrian death machine that underpins his account is
a descent into the unspeakable.

In 2014, Caesar testified before the House Foreign
Affairs Committee and his testimony provided crucial
evidence for a bipartisan bill, the Caesar Syria Civilian
Protection Act, which was presented to Congress in
2016. Caesar's photos have also been shown in the
United Nations Headquarters in New York and at the
Holocaust Memorial Museum in Washington, DC.

For the first time, this book tells Caesar's story.

Garance Le Caisne is an independent journalist. Having
lived in Cairo in the 1990s, she covered the Arab
Spring and travels regularly to Syria. Her articles
have appeared in publications including *Le Journal du
Dimanche* and *L'Obs*.

Operation Caesar

Operation Caesar

At the Heart of the Syrian
Death Machine

Garance Le Caisne

Translated by David Watson

polity

First published in French as *Opération César. Au coeur de la machine de mort syrienne* © Éditions Stock, 2015

This English edition © Polity Press, 2018

Polity Press
65 Bridge Street
Cambridge CB2 1UR, UK

Polity Press
101 Station Landing
Suite 300
Medford, MA 02155, USA

ISBN-13: 978-1-5095-2814-1
ISBN-13: 978-1-5095-2815-8 (pb)

A catalogue record for this book is available from the British Library.

Library of Congress Cataloging-in-Publication Data

Names: Le Caisne, Garance, author.
Title: Operation Caesar : at the heart of the Syrian death machine / Garance
    Le Caisne.
Other titles: Operation Cesar. English
Description: Cambridge, UK : Polity Press, 2018. | Includes bibliographical
    references and index.
Identifiers: LCCN 2017048526 (print) | LCCN 2017060772 (ebook) |
    ISBN 9781509528189 (Epub) | ISBN 9781509528141 |
    ISBN 9781509528141 (hardback) | ISBN 9781509528158 (pbk.)
Subjects: LCSH: Syria--History--Civil War, 2011---Atrocities. | War
    crimes--Syria--History--21st century. | Torture--Syria--History--21st
    century. | Prisoners of war--Abuse of--Syria--History--21st century. |
    Political violence--Syria--History--21st century. | Syria--History--Civil
    War, 2011---Personal narratives.
Classification: LCC DS98.6 (ebook) | LCC DS98.6 .L413 2018 (print) |
    DDC 956.9104/23--dc23
LC record available at https://lccn.loc.gov/2017048526

Typeset in 11 on 13pt Sabon
by Fakenham Prepress Solutions, Fakenham, Norfolk NR21 8NN
Printed and bound in Great Britain by CPI Group (UK) Ltd, Croydon

The publisher has used its best endeavours to ensure that the URLs for external websites referred to in this book are correct and active at the time of going to press. However, the publisher has no responsibility for the websites and can make no guarantee that a site will remain live or that the content is or will remain appropriate.

The publishers would like to thank the following for permission to reproduce the plates:
4: PHILIPPE DESMAZES/AFP/Getty Images
5: REUTERS/Lucas Jackson
6: Erkan Avci/Anadolu Agency/Getty Images

Every effort has been made to trace all copyright holders, but if any have been inadvertently overlooked the publisher will be pleased to include any necessary credits in any subsequent reprint or edition.

For further information on Polity, visit our website:
politybooks.com

To the men and women of Syria
To each of those numbers who were once
children, women, men
To their memory and that of their loved ones

'We have heard cries like this many times throughout history,
For a long time they rang out in vain,
And it was only later that they produced an echo.'

Gustawa Jarecka
Polish Jew from the Warsaw Ghetto
Member of the group Oyneg Shabes
December 1942

Contents

Prologue

When I looked at these photographs, they spoke to me. Many of the victims in these photos knew they were going to die. They had their finger raised as when you are about to die and you say the shahada.[1] *They had their mouths open in pain, and you could sense the humiliation they had suffered. Each time I looked at these faces, I could not erase them from my memory.*

They cried out in pain so that someone might save them, but no one saved them, no one listened to them. They asked for things, but no one heard.

Every day I heard the cries of victims expressing their suffering, telling us what goes on inside the prisons and detention centres. There was no one there to bear witness, no one replied. These victims have placed on my shoulders the responsibility to bear witness to their families, to humanity as whole and to the free world of the tortures inflicted upon them.

I left Syria with pure and sincere intentions. There are many files on the crimes of the regime: chemical attacks,

---

1 Muslim profession of faith: 'There is no God but God, and Muhammed is His Messenger.'

mass murder, detentions. All these files will be opened and used as evidence against Bashar al-Assad. When and how? I don't know.

The truth will lead to victory. There's a proverb that says: 'No right is lost as long as there is a person demanding it.'

Caesar, military police photographer in the Syrian regime of Bashar al-Assad, April 2015

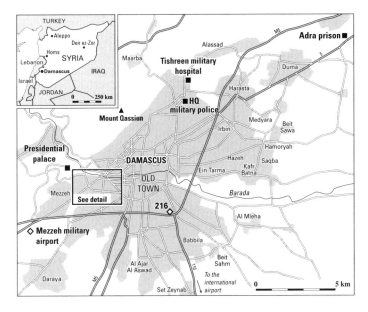

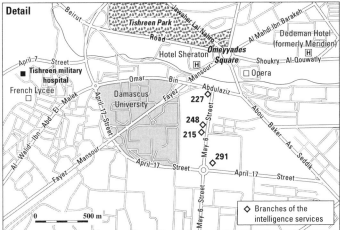

Locations where the witnesses of this book were detained

List of Syrians who bear witness in this book

Caesar is a former military photographer from Damascus whose job was to photograph the bodies of detainees who had died in detention centres and then archive the pictures in files. Horrified by this macabre routine, he decided to take copies of this evidence of the regime's brutality and smuggle them out of Syria so that the world could see. Caesar risked his life every day for two years.

Sami is a pseudonym. He is Caesar's closest friend. He is the person Caesar confided in and who would support him on a daily basis in his secret work until they escaped the country and took refuge in Europe.

Abu al-Leith is a pseudonym. Aged about thirty, this former shopkeeper from Qalamoun spent seven months in detention under the custody of Branch 227 of military intelligence, then in a cell in the civilian prison in Adra, nominally reserved for common-law criminals. He fled Syria for Turkey.

List of Syrians who bear witness in this book

Mazen al-Hummada was a technician working for a multinational oil firm based in Deir ez-Zor in the northeast of the country. Arrested three times for making videos of demonstrations and posting them online, he spent a year and a half in prison under the custody of Air Force intelligence, where he became a *soukhra*, the Arabic term for a forced labourer, tasked with helping his jailers in their everyday work, notably transporting bodies of dead detainees. He is currently based in the Netherlands.

Amer al-Homsi, a doctor from Homs, does not wish to be identified. He worked for fifteen years in the government hospital in the town. In 2011 and 2012 he saw the hospital turn into a sort of detention centre where wounded prisoners were tortured.

Munir Abu Muaz is a pseudonym. In two years of incarceration Munir, an engineer, was transferred between four branches of two different security services, then was sent to Saydnaya, thirty kilometres from Damascus, a prison reserved for political detainees and Islamists, a worthy successor to the one at Palmyra. He spent several weeks in the military hospital at Mezzeh. He currently lives in Turkey.

Ahmad al-Riz joined the revolution at the age of twenty-five. He learned how to encrypt messages on the internet and secretly organize mass gatherings. He was arrested and was held by different branches for seven months before being moved to Saydnaya prison. He received treatment twice in Tishreen military hospital. He sought refuge in Germany, where he is learning the language in order to pursue his studies.

Wafa is a pseudonym. Arrested along with her husband in May 2013, she was freed in a prisoner exchange four and a half months later. Her husband died under torture. She found the photo of his body among those that Caesar smuggled out.

Ahmed comes from a family in Daraya, a suburb of the capital, which was in the forefront of the peaceful revolution. He wishes to preserve his family name as he awaits the opportunity to lodge a case against Bashar al-Assad. His brother and his uncle were tortured to death by Air Force intelligence. Their photos appear in Caesar's files.

Abu Khaled, commander of a katiba in the mountains of Qalamoun. This slightly built, taciturn individual organized Caesar's escape in summer 2013. He also smuggled out of Syria the hard drive containing the 53,000 original photos.

Hassan al-Shalabi, political activist and founder member of the Syrian National Movement who was forced to flee Syria. He followed Operation Caesar from abroad and brought the files to international attention.

Imad Eddine al-Rachid, former vice-dean of the Faculty of Sharia in Damascus, head of the Syrian National Movement. He tried to convince the United States to send Bashar al-Assad to face trial at the International Criminal Court. In July 2014, Imad accompanied Caesar to Washington, where the former photographer addressed Congress.

Imran is a pseudonym. This young IT specialist in his twenties comes originally from Moadamyeh in the suburbs of Damascus. Pursued by the regime, he sought refuge in Turkey. He worked with Sami to log the thousands of photographs in order to make the files accessible to everyone.

Zakaria is a pseudonym. Formerly a paediatrician in Damascus, he fled Syria for Lebanon before going to Turkey. Using Caesar's photos, he has drawn up a medical list of all the abuses the victims were subjected to.

Foreword

This English translation of Garance Le Caisne's riveting account of *Operation Caesar* arrives at a critical moment in the history of Syria's brutal civil war. After almost seven years of conflict, the regime of Bashar al-Assad is on the cusp of crushing the insurgency that emerged in early 2011, initially as a response to the violence it unleashed against millions of Syrians who had taken to the streets demanding freedom, justice and dignity. Over time, the exuberance and optimism of Syria's revolution morphed into something far darker, twisted in part by the skill with which the Assad regime corrupted the uprising's original peaceful impulses and the ruthlessness with which it defended its hold on power.

As the regime's victory draws closer, the world confronts a stark choice: to remember or to forget. To look past the atrocities and crimes committed by the Assad regime, or to insist that Assad and his accomplices be held responsible for the unimaginable horrors they inflicted on the people of Syria.

Displaying victor's arrogance, the Assad regime and its allies in Russia and Iran consider amnesia and accommodation their due. They appeal both to pragmatism and to greed, dangling the promise of rewards in the form of reconstruction contracts to supplicants, while threatening retribution to those who continue to press for accountability. Such efforts, they argue, are pointless. Assad's fate, after all, is secure. Normalization of the Assad regime is inevitable. Accept it and move on.

The narrative that Le Caisne presents in the following pages is a compelling and powerful rebuttal of these claims. The extraordinary story of Caesar, an unwitting archivist of the systematic torture and murder of thousands of Syrians, demands that we reckon with the price of pragmatism and the cost of forgetting. To confront the searing, first-hand account of his experiences as a military photographer charged with recording victims of regime brutality, alongside those of his associates and the scarred survivors of detention in regime torture chambers, brings us face-to-face with the cruelty that lies at the core of Assad's regime. The violence recorded in these pages was not an unfortunate byproduct of war. It was systematic and intentional, a matter of bureaucratic protocols and standard operating procedures. To accommodate the regime's demand for amnesia is not merely to condone its routinization of torture, but to consign its current and future victims to a similar fate.

Worse, perhaps, is that we knew and did not act. Even Caesar's testimony before the US Congress, and public displays of his photographs of brutalized victims at the United Nations and the UK House of Commons, were not sufficient to induce governments to act. Now, with the approaching defeat of Syria's uprising, governments that lent half-hearted support to the opposition are anxious to justify their policies of non-intervention, their willingness to hollow out and render facile their commitment to 'never again'. To forget, however, will compound the crimes of the Assad regime and deepen the wounds of its victims in their hundreds of thousands. If the publication of *Operation Caesar* in English makes it that much more difficult, that much less comfortable, for those complicit in inaction to become complicit in forgetting, it will have achieved a great deal.

Caesar has helped restore dignity to those whom the regime mutilated and murdered. Through Le Caisne's painstakingly researched account, they are recovered from anonymity and made visible to us as human beings. The photographs that Caesar smuggled out of Syria, and the personal stories that he learned from relatives and loved ones of the regime's victims, are as important as the individual narratives to emerge from other experiences of mass killing, from the Holocaust to Cambodia to Rwanda. Like the perpetrators of previous mass atrocities, the Assad regime carries a stain that can never be erased. The legacies of the pain and trauma it inflicted have not diminished. They remain alive with survivors, and with the families of those who did not survive. They will become the inheritance of their children and their children's children. We may wish to avert our gaze. *Operation Caesar* requires us to look, to pay attention, to remember.

Steven Heydemann
Janet W. Ketcham Chair in Middle East Studies
Smith College

Preface

In spring 2014, when an editor suggested I should track down Caesar, the reasons were self-evident. This man, a former Syrian military photographer, had smuggled out evidence of crimes against humanity in a way in which no one else had dared do. At that time everyone in the media had heard of this individual who had copied thousands of documents and photos of dead detainees in the regime's jails from a military police computer in Damascus.

For two years, this anonymous hero copied images of tortured, starved, burned bodies with numbers marked on their flesh. Pictures that his superiors had asked him to take, to document and record the death of prisoners, and that he had transferred onto memory sticks in order to smuggle them out, hidden inside his shoe or his belt.

The terrorists of Islamic State flaunted their barbarity all over social media. The Syrian state hid theirs in the silence of their prison cells. Before this there had been no eye-witness accounts from the inside of the Syrian death machine in action. These photographs and documents were devastating.

The group that had been helping Caesar and trying to alert Western governments and the international media had recently visited Paris. One of their leaders had given me an interview for *Le Journal du Dimanche* on 'the archivist of horror'.

Around this time, the photographer Laurence Geai and I were preparing a news story in Aleppo, which would be published in the summer of 2014 in *Le Nouvel Observateur*. In parts of the city held by the opposition we had witnessed the willingness of the regime to crush a section of its own people and to bury their memory. One Wednesday morning, in the space of two hours, three bombs fell less than 200 metres away from us. We witnessed the death of a young man with whom we had been laughing the night before and whom we were going to follow that day as part of our story. We saw flesh ripped to shreds. Barrel bombs of TNT dropped by helicopters from the army of Bashar al-Assad, the rushed burial of body parts. And especially the graves dug by the men from the morgue to bury the bodies that hadn't been claimed.

It had become a matter of some urgency to track down Caesar. The spectacular gains made by Islamic State (Daesh) and the increase in terrorist attacks by those affiliated with them were drowning out the revelations of atrocities on the part of the Syrian regime. The conflict had already claimed more than 220,000 deaths. Half the civilian population had been made homeless. Others were being shelled and put under siege by the loyalist army.

Caesar could bring the abuses of the Damascus regime back to centre stage. He had to be found. The former Syrian military photographer was being sought by journalists around the world. I knew it would be difficult, and it was. Twice I had almost given up. Twice I took up the quest again, because it was simply unconscionable that this man shouldn't talk. His testimony was crucial for understanding the horror of this regime. It was essential that his account should complement the publication of the photos. I constantly had the memory of Aleppo before me, its nameless graves, and other photos, these ones discovered in the morgue set up in a former girls' school.

In a classroom, dozens of pictures of Aleppans killed in shelling by the regime were stuck to the walls. As you entered this room and saw this before your eyes, the portraits of Cambodians exterminated by the Khmer Rouge and displayed in a former school in Phnom Penh suddenly superimposed themselves. Between 1975 and 1979 more than 17,000 people died in S21, the largest centre of torture of Pol Pot's regime. Today, photos of the victims are displayed in the location, which has now been turned into a museum.

The members of the group who were protecting Caesar and who belonged to the Syrian National Movement, a moderate Islamist opposition party, understood that this book would not be merely a media scoop but rather a descent into the unspeakable. That it would give a voice to Syrians and leave a trace for future generations.

We met on several occasions. In Paris, France, in Istanbul, Turkey, in Jeddah, Saudi Arabia. They opened their files, their documents, and told their own stories. But when it came to meeting up with Caesar I always hit a brick wall. I didn't know why, I just knew that the man was afraid. Disappointed at the inertia of the international community, he wasn't seeing eye to eye with the leaders of the group. He had been hiding, indeed was still in hiding, fearing for his safety.

However, this book couldn't happen without his testimony. And then a member of the group allowed a preliminary interview with Sami. Unbeknown to the media who had followed the 'Caesar affair', Sami was the one who knew the most about the former military photographer. He had accompanied him and supported him during the two years of the operation. He was the key to getting access to Caesar.

We spoke on four different occasions, each time for several hours. Accompanied by Saoussen Ben Cheikh, who translated for me, we spent time with him and his wife and got along well. Surprisingly, movingly at times, a relationship of trust blossomed between us. One evening Sami had to reassure Caesar. Thanks to the internet, Skype had been the tool of communication between Syrian activists since the start of the Revolution and the war. It was secure and free. Sami and I were in the habit of talking to each other without connecting our webcams.

'Caesar is worried, he's afraid,' Sami explained. 'Some lawyers are pressuring him to give testimony before the public prosecutors. Can they force him to?' I knew nothing about the ins and outs of international justice but I could reassure them on a couple of things at least: there would be no policeman coming to arrest him and drag him in front of a judge. Caesar and Sami were no longer living under the Syrian dictatorship but in a democracy in northern Europe where they had sought refuge. Nevertheless, they should not forget the reason why they had risked their lives and those of their families. Why they had fled their country to go to another one where they didn't speak the language.

This is how I put it: 'One day, it will be necessary for Caesar to give testimony on the crimes of the regime, on what he has witnessed, on what he was forced to do. For the Syrian people, for justice. Maybe not today, if he is too afraid, but tomorrow, the day after tomorrow, in six months' time, a year from now, he will have to do it. Do you understand, Sami?' Silence. Then, all of a sudden, an unfamiliar voice. Someone I didn't know, whom I couldn't see, seemed to be sitting next to Sami: 'Hello. Thank you for your advice. I am Caesar. You can see me whenever you like.'

After six months of searching, he had agreed to show himself. As was the case with Sami, our first encounter was a little tense. Them on the defensive, me afraid of 'losing' them if I put my questions the wrong way, if I asked for too many details too quickly, too soon. Caesar confided in me on several occasions. Put end to end, our exchanges lasted more than forty hours.

The testimony he offered me is unique. In simple words, without ever claiming to have done or seen anything he hadn't done or seen, Caesar described his work in painstaking detail. He made sketches to explain himself more clearly. On a satellite map he showed me the journey he made every day; he showed me the hangars at one of the military hospitals where he had to photograph the corpses. As these interviews went on he opened up more, but quite often he would become reticent and keep his emotions to himself. His safety had been an overriding concern to him from the beginning. The pages he wrote on stayed in his possession: it was out of the question that his writing should be revealed. He left me just one drawing. To reassure him, we decided between us to reveal nothing about his private life. We have even altered a few details.

The photographers of the Syrian military police are just one link in the chain of death. They take pictures of corpses for the records. To complete my understanding of Caesar's confession it was necessary to meet some of the survivors of torture at the detention centres, prisons and military hospitals. Those who had witnessed the deaths of cellmates or patients in adjacent beds. Those who had had to carry the bodies. Those who saw the numbers marked onto the corpses. They bear witness here, their faces covered or under pseudonyms.

The collection of evidence of crimes committed in Syria, begun by a handful of people seven years ago, is still in its early stages. In its own way, this book is a first attempt to tell the truth. The inquest will continue.

Despite Caesar's revelations, the International Criminal Court is unable to pursue the regime for its crimes, hamstrung as it is by the opposition of Russia, an ally of the Syrian regime. As the international system is stymied, national jurisdictions have to take on the mantle of seeking justice.

Since this book was first published in French in 2015, several complaints have been lodged in Europe against leading players in the regime, with the Caesar file at the centre of these investigations. This involves long, delicate but essential work on the part of lawyers. They have to persuade surviving detainees to testify, smuggle the families of the plaintiffs out of Syria to protect them from reprisals, convince national legal authorities to accept politically sensitive litigation ...

In Germany a number of Syrian refugees, supported by the European Centre for Constitutional and Human Rights (ECCHR), have taken action in the German courts against members of the regime for war crimes and crimes against humanity. On 20 September 2017, high-resolution files of the original 53,000 photos were sent by Sami to the German Public Prosecutor General in Karlsruhe. They will now be thoroughly analysed to confirm the facts.

In France, on the advice of the human rights organization Fédération internationale des droits de l'homme (FIDH), a Franco-Syrian engineer went to court in October 2016 over the arbitrary arrest and forced disappearance of his brother and his nephew in Damascus.

In Spain the law firm Guernica 37 lodged a case with the public prosecutor in February 2017 concerning the death of a delivery driver in one of the regime's detention centres. Their client, the man's sister, now a naturalized Spanish citizen, recognized his body among Caesar's photos. The prosecutor declined jurisdiction, but Guernica 37 have appealed. 'Because it must not be forgotten that, even before the outbreak of the armed conflict, the regime was killing its citizens like rats and is still doing do,' states the pugnacious Almudena Bernabeu, the Guernica 37 lawyer.

Memory and justice. Justice and memory.

Numbers, photos. Emaciated corpses. It is something we have seen before. The revelations of Caesar's photos remind me of the extermination of the Jews in the Shoah, even if it is history and justice that will qualify the crimes of the Syrian regime.

Many of the images are simply too horrifying to print. Readers might be unable or unwilling to read the testimonies of the survivors after viewing them. In consultation with the publisher of this English edition, we have decided to include a small number of carefully selected photos to give some idea of the brutality that Caesar witnessed. Further images can be viewed in the report commissioned by Human Rights Watch, available at: https://www.hrw.org/news/2015/12/16/syria-stories-behind-photos-killed-detainees

This book is an account of the everyday barbarity of the regime Bashar al-Assad has imposed on the Syrian people. This is their story.

I
Revelation. Testimony. Accusation

Diplomats, advisors, collaborators all have to leave the room. An ultra-sensitive file is about to be opened for the eyes only of the eleven foreign ministers present. A file in the form of an eight-minute video. On a wide-screen TV, the film begins. Voice off: 'This film contains shocking and horrifying scenes, committed by the Syrian regime. These are some examples of the tens of thousands of official photographs that we have received, the authenticity of which we have confirmed through judicial means, original documents and eyewitness testimonies. Experts in legal procedure have confirmed the validity of the evidence and the reliability of the source. Consequently, we present this report with complete confidence.'

That Sunday, 12 January 2014, in the Second Empire dining room at the Ministry of Foreign Affairs in Paris, Laurent Fabius was hosting his foreign counterparts: John Kerry, the US Secretary of State, and diplomatic heads from Egypt, Germany, Italy, Jordan, Qatar, Saudi Arabia, Turkey, the United Arab Emirates and the United Kingdom.

The Core Group of the Friends of Syria had gathered together to support Ahmad Jarba, president of the

Syrian National Coalition, the main representative of the political opposition. The opposition and the Syrian regime were due to meet ten days later in Switzerland to discuss the creation of a transitional government, but the members of the Coalition were divided about whether to participate in these international peace talks, which were set to open in Montreux and continue in Geneva under the aegis of the UN. The eleven Friends of the Syrian People wanted the Coalition to be involved so that Bashar al-Assad could not lay the blame for the failure of these discussions at the door of the opposition.

The French foreign minister, who was chairing the discussion, took his seat at the centre of the table, opposite Ahmad Jarba. At the end of the morning session, unexpectedly, he invited Khaled al-Attiyah to speak. A few days earlier, the Qatari minister had informed him that an opposition group had brought him a confidential document that he wished to show them. The talks were suspended. About thirty people left the room. Only the eleven foreign ministers remained around the table.

The lights were dimmed. Against the background of music composed by Itzhak Perlman for the film *Schindler's List*, a series of photos played across the screen: bodies, naked, stripped to underpants or in rags. Skeletal corpses, some of them mutilated, lacerated or burned. Some had had their eyes torn out. Others were disfigured by some chemical substance. Others, finally, were wrapped in black plastic and piled under the porch of a hangar. The camera scrupulously lingered on the numbers each of these cadavers bore, either marked in indelible ink on their flesh or written on a label stuck to their forehead. This macabre gallery had clearly been photographed by a professional. In the gilded surroundings of the Foreign Ministry, the audience watched in silence, frozen in horror.

The voiceover continued: 'Rarely in history have such acts of systematic deprivation of food and brutal torture within detention centres of the Syrian regime been documented in this way. From death shortly after arrest to the physical liquidation of detainees within prisons or military hospitals, the regime archived cases of death through photos taken by the criminal department of the military police ... The medical records state that they died of heart attacks, yet the bodies show signs of torture and famine.' The film ended with: 'Is this a new Holocaust? It is still going on today.'

The ministers filed out without saying a word, faces serious. John Kerry was ashen. The lunch that followed was barely touched. Laurent Fabius told his team: 'It's awful, horrific. We have to get to the truth of all these documents; they are of vital importance.'

'These images corroborated what France had been saying for years about the regime of Bashar al-Assad', said a source close to Fabius, speaking more recently. 'Images we haven't seen since the Jewish genocide and the crimes of the Khmer Rouge. The sophisticated manner in which the Syrian regime documents and classifies its crimes takes us back sixty years.'

At the end of the day, sitting before a microphone at the press conference, Laurent Fabius referred publicly to the underlying principle of the Geneva 2 conference, to arrive at 'a real political transition that brings an end to the present despotic regime ... while respecting the sovereignty of the Syrian people'. Then, grim-faced, the French foreign minister emphasized 'our utter condemnation of the atrocities perpetrated by the Syrian regime against its own people and in particular the atrocities committed recently. We know that, contrary to what we hear repeatedly, there is not the regime of Bashar al-Assad on one side and the terrorists on the other, but that it is this regime that nurtures terrorism, and if we want to be rid of the terrorism we must ensure that this regime is brought to an end.'

The Risk of Assassination

The day after this meeting, 5,000 kilometres away, in Doha, Qatar, another meeting was taking place. This one was completely secret. Since the start of the Revolution, this small Persian Gulf state had been supporting opponents of the Syrian regime, particularly those of an Islamist tendency. When the Qatari foreign minister learned of the existence of the photos and saw twenty or so of them spread out on his desk, he didn't hesitate to stand by the Syrian National Movement. It was the rebels of the National Movement, a moderate Islamist tendency, politically open and socially conservative, who were protecting the man who smuggled these tens of thousands of photos out of Syria.

Aware that its ferocious opposition to Bashar al-Assad risked jeopardizing the credibility of the file, Qatar commissioned the London law firm Carter-Ruck and Co. to validate the photos and accredit the source. The law firm engaged three former international lawyers and three experts in medical anthropology to draw up a report in order to interpret the numbers that appeared on the bodies and to do a scientific analysis of the pictures. Vital information for when the time came to reveal the file to the public.

So on 13 January 2014, in a private room in a luxury hotel in Doha, two of these lawyers were sitting at a table in front of two memory cards. The American David Crane and the Briton Desmond de Silva knew each other well: they had both in turn headed up the special tribunal for Sierra Leone which tried and sentenced the Liberian president Charles Taylor for war crimes and crimes against humanity.

4

The two former lawyers had come to Qatar to interrogate the source, who was still in hiding. The man was a deserter from the Syrian army. He had arrived in Doha the day before. Sitting next to an interpreter and opposite David Crane and Desmond de Silva, he accepted what to him seemed like an interrogation with good grace. He often felt ill at ease in his lightweight jacket; his gaze was troubled. They sometimes had to repeat questions as he didn't grasp what was meant the first time. His short replies, his simple, economical use of words showed him to be a reserved character, scarcely aware of the heroic nature of the operation he had undertaken. It was a modesty and calm that he never deviated from.

'Did you hand over these photos of your own free will?' Desmond de Silva asked.

'Yes. I did it as a service to Syria. To the loved ones of the detainees among the Syrian people', the man replied.

[...]

'I have a simple question. Why did you do it?' David Crane asked in turn.

'For the Syrians, for the people. So that the murderers should be held accountable for their crimes and judged for them', the man said.

'So you did all this for the sake of justice. So that justice will be done in the end.'

'Yes, I did it for the sake of justice.'

'To hold to account the people who did this?'

'Yes, those who are in charge of the military branches of the regime.'

[...]

'Was it very dangerous for you to copy these photos?' asked Desmond de Silva.

'Yes, very dangerous.'

'If the authorities had discovered these photos on you, you would have been in big trouble?'

'Yes, me, my family and everyone who knows me.'

'Now you are here, you left Syria. Why did you leave and how?'

'I left because I was afraid for myself and my family. If the security services had found out that I had copied the photos, we would have been punished by death.'

'So you decided to leave Syria. Who helped you to leave Syria?'

'I crossed the border illegally.'

'Did you receive any money in exchange for this?' Desmond de Silva continued.

'No.'

'So you derived no personal benefit from this?' David Crane insisted.

'No.'

'You did all this out of conscience?'

'*Inch'Allah*. How can I ensure my safety, in your opinion?' the man asked worriedly. His voice was soft, but his anxiety was obvious.

'You are safe here', Desmond de Silva assured him. 'We will not show your photo or divulge your name in our reports. That's why we have given you the codename "Caesar".'

2

Profession Corpse Photographer

Caesar

'I am Caesar. I used to work for the Syrian regime. I was a photographer with the military police in Damascus. I will describe my work before the Revolution and during the first two years of the Revolution. But I can't include everything, because I am scared that the regime might be able to identify me by the details that I divulge. I escaped to Europe. I am afraid that they will find me and eliminate me, or subject my family to reprisals.

'Before the Revolution, my job was to take photographs of crime and accident scenes that involved the military. These might be suicides, drownings, road accidents, house fires. I and the other service photographers would have to visit the scene and photograph the location, the victims. Once there, we would be instructed by the judge or investigating officer: "Photograph such and such a person. Take a picture of this." Our work complemented theirs. For example, if there had been a crime committed in an office, we would photograph the place where the body had been found, then we would photograph the body itself at the morgue to show where the bullet had entered and the exit wound. We might also photograph the crime-scene evidence, a pistol or a knife. If it was a road accident, we would photograph the location, the car. We would take all this back to the office, where a report would be drawn up, accompanied by our photos. Then the report would be sent to military justice so that the judicial process could get under way.

'Back then, a lot of regular and conscript soldiers were keen to join the service. Many wanted to be posted there because there wasn't a huge workload. There was maybe one case every two or three days. And you weren't forced to wear a uniform; you could choose to work in either uniform or civvies.

'But it didn't appeal so much to the officers! Of course, commanding a bunch of photographers and archivists doesn't have much prestige. The military police doesn't have much authority in the country, as opposed to the intelligence services. What's more, we had no contact with the civil authorities, so there was no possibility of making money out of bribes, the way they do in the Customs and the ministries. And we had no influence on the security services and the army.

'In the military hierarchy our work was largely overlooked; we didn't really count. We were just one among dozens of others. The military police is made up of dozens of different departments, branches and battalions. In Damascus alone there are about thirty different services: photographers, drivers, mechanics … operations, sport, prisoner transportation between the different branches of military intelligence. But the most important were the investigation and prison services.

'One day, a colleague told me we were to photograph some civilian bodies. He had just been to photograph the corpses of protestors in the province of Deraa:[1] It was in the first few weeks of the Revolution, in March or April 2011. In tears, he told me: "The soldiers desecrated the bodies. They were stamping on them with their boots and shouting 'sons of whores!'"

'My colleague didn't want to go back, he was afraid. When it was my turn to go, I saw for myself. The officers were describing them as "terrorists". But they weren't, they were simply protestors. The bodies were being kept in the morgue at Tishreen military hospital, a hospital not far from military police headquarters.

'At first, the person's name was attached to their body. After a while, maybe a few weeks or a month, the bodies didn't have names any more. Just numbers. At the morgue in Tishreen hospital, a soldier would take them out of the refrigerated cabinets, lay them on the tiles so that we could photograph them, then put them back in the drawers.

'Whenever we were called in for a photo session a medical examiner was already there. Like us, the forensics staff were not obliged to wear a uniform, but they had military ranks. In the first few months they were simply middle-ranking officers. Later, these were replaced by the top brass.

'When they arrived at the hospital, the bodies had two numbers attached to them. These were written on Scotch tape or marked in felt-tip on their skin, on their forehead or chest. The tape was not of good quality and often peeled off. The first was the number of the prisoner himself, the second referred to the branch of the intelligence services where he had been imprisoned. The medical examiner would come early in the morning and assign a third number to them, relating to his

---

1   The region in the south of the country where the first large (and peaceful) demonstrations broke out.

medical report. This number was the most important one for our records. The other two might be badly written, illegible or simply inaccurate, as mistakes were not uncommon. The medical examiner wrote the medical number on a piece of cardboard. He or a security services agent would hold this up next to the body as we photographed it. It is their hands that you see on the photos I smuggled out. Sometimes you can even see the feet of the medical examiner or the agent next to the body.

'The medical examiners were our superiors. We weren't allowed to speak, never mind ask questions. When one of them gave us an order, we had to obey. They would say: "Photograph these bodies, numbers 1 to 30, for example, then you can go." So that they could be readily identified in the dossiers, we had to take several pictures of each body: one of the face, one of the whole body, one from the side, one of head and shoulders, one of the legs.

'The bodies were grouped according to the branches. For example, there was one place for Branch 215 of military intelligence, another for Air Force intelligence. This made it easier to take the photographs and classify them later.

'I had never seen this before. Before the Revolution, the regime would torture people to extract information. Now they were simply torturing people to death. I saw the candle burns. Once I saw a round mark made by an electric element – the sort you use to heat up tea – which had been used to burn someone's face and hair. Some people had deep knife wounds, eyeballs ripped out, broken teeth, whip marks from car jump leads. There were bruises filled with pus, as if they had not been tended for a long time and had got infected. Sometimes, the bodies were covered in blood, and the blood was still fresh. That meant that they had died recently.

'I had to take breaks so that I wouldn't start crying. I would go off and wash my face. I was no better at home. I had changed. I'm normally quite calm, but I would fly off the handle with my parents, my brothers and my sisters. I was simply terrified. The things I had seen during the day would pass before my eyes. I could picture my brothers and sisters as one of those corpses. It made me ill.

'I couldn't take any more, so I decided to talk to Sami, a friend. We lived in the same area.'

Confiding in a Friend

Sami
One evening in spring 2011, Caesar went to see Sami. He was very agitated. In Sami's living-room he whispered.

'I have to tell you about some weird things that are happening at work.'

'What is it?'

'I've seen bodies that have been tortured. They didn't die of natural causes. And there are more and more of them every day.' In tears, Caesar asked imploringly: 'What should I do?'

The families of Caesar and Sami had known each other for more than twenty years. The two men had been close for a few years and saw each other regularly. But in the Syria of Assad Senior and Junior there were certain things you didn't talk about, things you didn't dare criticize even in a whisper to your friends and family. The cult of the president, for example, the suppression of all political opposition, the complete absence of freedom, the intelligence services, who monitor every detail of citizens' lives, who control every corner of the city. One word out of place could land you in jail. The regime maintains its grip through terror, oppression.

Sami was a construction engineer in Damascus. He knew that Caesar had been posted to an office of the military police where they photograph road accidents and military deaths. Sami had always taken just a mild interest. Until he was stung by these latest confidences, that is.

In this year, 2011, after Tunisia, Egypt and Libya, the Syrians started to demand their Arab spring. Two early demonstrations in February and the beginning of March put Damascus on the back foot. A call to join the protests went out on Facebook on 15 March, and three days later, on Friday 18 March, in Deraa, in the rural and tribal south, looked down on by the metropolitan elites, thousands of people gathered before the great mosque. A few days earlier children in the town had dared to write on the walls of their school: 'The people want the fall of the regime.' Arrested, tortured, they were completely unrecognizable when returned to their parents with the sheer contempt the security services felt for a people they imagined to be subjugated, ignorant and broken by forty-five years of the arbitrary exercise of power.

But something happened. With a strength they barely thought themselves still capable of, Syrians marched peacefully against the arrests and demanded reforms. Deraa, normally a bastion of the ruling Baath party, decided it had had enough of being marginalized by Damascus and dominated by an oligarchy which helped itself to what scant economic resources there were in the region. The demonstration of 18 March was put down within the hour, and three young people were killed.

Immediately, other peaceful protests sprang up across the region and the rest of the country. With the slogans loud in their ears, the soldiers clamped down hard. Most of the protestors dispersed, but some carried on. In the days that followed, the doors of mosques witnessed a quick succession of funerals of martyrs who had been cut down, the bodies carried wrapped in a flag, sometimes covered with flowers, with ever-larger crowds of rebels proclaiming 'Wahed, wahed!' ('One, the people are one!')

Syrians began to speak out in public, defying their fear. Many would fall. In their thousands, opponents of the regime posted videos of peaceful assemblies on the internet. YouTube and Facebook accounts were inundated with hundreds of sequences showing victims lying in agony on the pavement, fathers weeping over their bloodied sons, mothers wailing. White shrouds being lowered into the ground.

The filming was for those who lived at the other end of the country. To break the censorship. To pay homage to those slaughtered in the repression.

Three decades earlier, in the town of Hama, 15,000 to 25,000 inhabitants had been killed: shot against a wall, crushed by tanks, thrown out of windows, killed on arriving at hospital. Machine-gunned with no witnesses present. Shattered lives, many without a grave, without tributes or remembrance. Disappeared. In February 1982 the regime wanted to put down an insurrection by the Muslim Brotherhood in this town in the centre of the country. The elite troops of Rifat al-Assad, brother of Hafez al-Assad, the then president, led the battle. Several weeks of collective punishment destroyed a third of the town. No photographs, no films. Silent witnesses, paralysed families. But throughout the country the sound of shells had sown terror.

For a long time in the maze of the old town of Hama or around the new hotels built on top of mass graves, the inhabitants shied away from talking about these events. Their memories were silent, but they were intact. Like that October evening in 2014 in Brussels, when, at the end of a conference on Aleppo, a Syrian woman who had grown up in Hama shed tears as she recounted how, as a little girl, elsewhere at the time of the massacres, she had returned one month later to find a ghost town and her family partially decimated. She hadn't been able to talk about it for years. Until now, jogged by the images of the streets and mosques of Hama before the destruction, her childhood agony was reawoken.

Adolescent Fear, Adult Terror

At the time of the events in Hama, Sami was still at school. 'The terrorists will come and murder us in school', the adults told him, referring to the Muslim Brotherhood. In the evenings the teachers organized vigils to protect the people of the neighbourhood. Sami saw his classmates disappear, one after the other. Why? How? Best not to ask too many questions. Arrested by the intelligence services, some returned. Others didn't, like his friend, a good, hard-working student, of whom he still awaits news – thirty-three years later.

One morning, after a song in honour of the president, Hafez al-Assad, the headmaster came into the school yard, surrounded by henchmen from the security forces. Sami and his classmates, lined up and ready to go in for their class in Islamic education, froze. Their teacher was an old man, whom the pupils loved and respected. The armed henchmen started insulting him, threatened to rape his wife: 'You'll learn to pay the price for opposing your superiors', they barked. And then they took him away.

'His arrest was a terrifying moment, more terrifying than painful', Sami recalls. 'I thought of him as a sort of father. I realized that we weren't living in a country but in a vast prison. I didn't feel safe any more, I could no longer concentrate on my studies. I spoke about it to my mother. To protect me, she asked me to forget about it and never talk about what had just happened.'

He had to be careful of what he said even with his closest friends. In the evening, when they sat up together and talked about Assad, the boys couldn't mention the forename Hafez without attaching the title of president. If one of their friends had been an agent of intelligences services or the Baath party, that would be the end of the one who 'showed disrespect' to the leader.

Twenty-nine years later, looking at the first photos that Caesar had copied, Sami relived those fears of his youth. 'I realized that there were people dying in silence in the prisons. They were in the regime's dark holes.' There was torture before the Revolution. People coming out of prison, sometimes after twenty years of arbitrary detention, told stories about it. The regime was happy to have these accounts disseminated to serve as examples, so that they could sow terror in every home, every mind.

But Caesar's photos showed torture and death listed and classified by the regime. This time it is the state itself telling the story of the terror it is inflicting. Taken in the dungeons of the military hospitals, these images are irrefutable evidence of the barbarity of power. As opposed to the amateur films, full of emotion, that the activists for freedom shot in the streets of the cities, these official documents chill the blood.

Caesar wanted to leave his job and defect. Sami listened to him and persuaded him to carry on, as he alone was able to gather evidence from inside the system. He promised to support him and stick by him, whatever happened. These two men, so different in many ways, would become inseparable. Sami, so proud of his culture and his origins, but shaped by four decades of dictatorship, was often distrustful and suspicious. His piercing eyes and hard expression were difficult to read. Occasionally his face would be lit up by a smile, revealing sensitive feelings he normally sought to conceal. Caesar was more direct and expressed himself in simple, honest language, rather like a child. His words had no ulterior meaning. He spoke as plainly as possible, never employing metaphor to colour his speech. For two years, at great personal risk, the young photographer copied thousands of photos of detainees, which can now be viewed on the internet, and some of which are projected in a room in the Holocaust Museum in Washington in the USA. Sami supported him on a daily basis throughout those two years. He is still supporting him, somewhere in Northern Europe, where the two men now live in hiding. Waiting for judicial procedure to take its course, they are unable to reveal their true identities while the Assad regime remains in place.

3

The Routine Turns to Horror

Caesar

'At one point the bodies were also sent to military hospital at Mezzeh, which is much bigger than the one at Tishreen. Its real name is Hospital 601. Tishreen was just five minutes by car from our office; Mezzeh was about fifteen kilometres away, a half hour by car.

'It was easier to photograph the bodies at Tishreen, because they were placed out of the light and the sun, in the morgue or in the corridors when the morgue was full. At Mezzeh they were left outside, on the ground, in one of the garages where the cars were serviced and repaired. The hospital is at the foot of the hill where the Presidential Guard is. On some of the photos you can see the hill, with the sentry box of the hospital guard and the trees that mark the boundary of the establishment. The presidential palace is just behind that, higher up.

'I saw bodies of Christians and Alawites.[1] I saw one

---

1 A religious sect of the Assad clan, a minority group in the country, constituting just 10–12% of the population. An offshoot of the main Shia tradition, the Alawite Muslims

who had the face of Bashar al-Assad tattooed on his chest as a mark of allegiance.

'Along with my colleagues, my job was not only to photograph the bodies but also to make a file on them. We had to print the photos, arrange them branch by branch, attach them to forms and classify them. It was all very methodical: one person would print the photos, another would stick or clip them to the forms, a third would write up the reports. Our superiors would sign them off and then they were sent to military justice. Before the Revolution, we did this work on military corpses. After, we did the same work but with civilians. The same routine.

'The numbers increased. Especially after 2012. Then there was no stopping. The officer in charge of our service would shout at us: "Why haven't you finished yet?! The bodies are piling up! Get a move on!" He thought we were slacking, but it was impossible to go any faster. There were always more bodies to deal with, and there were fewer of us because of desertions. We were under such pressure that, in the end, the bodies began to agglutinate in the garage at Mezzeh before we had time to photograph them.

'Out there, in the sun and the heat, the bodies weren't well preserved, especially when they were left there more than two days. Even the soldiers didn't want to touch them, they pushed them with the toes of their boots, showing no respect.

'They were decomposing. One day we saw a bird peck the eyeball out of a corpse. Other times, there

---

are largely concentrated in Syria. Along with other Shiites, they revere Ali, the son-in-law of Muhammad, whom they consider to be the guide of the community, deriving his authority from God. So the Prophet himself occupies a secondary place, which is not the case with the Sunnis.

would be insects attacking the flesh. Then there was the smell. Not at Tishreen hospital, because they were kept inside, but at the hospital at Mezzeh, in the outdoor garage. That smell, which we couldn't get rid of at the start, drove us mad. We had to live with it every day of our lives.

'We worked from 8 a.m. until 2 p.m., then had a break until 6 or 7 p.m. Then, when we got back to the office, from 7 to 10 p.m. They were long days; we had to work in the evenings so as not to fall behind. We knew that there would be more bodies to photograph the next day.'

A Form for Each Dead Person

Like the countries in the former Soviet Bloc, every piece of information and documentation in Syria is classified and recorded. A state that doubts the fidelity of its minions likes to keep lists to avoid any mishaps. In the apparatus of the Syrian regime, no one trusts anyone. It's not enough to obey orders, you have to demonstrate that you have carried them out properly. Officers ask their juniors to account for themselves, which they are eager to do for fear of being labelled as insubordinate, cowardly or something else, charges that can lead to imprisonment without trial. Do detainees die of starvation or under torture in the detention centres of the intelligence services? It's a secret, but it's recorded and documented. With doctored death certificates showing death by natural causes.

A Hyundai pulls up in the courtyard of the military hospital in Mezzeh, in the centre of Damascus, and almost immediately two soldiers throw out ten or so naked bodies onto the ground. 'Chuck those sons of bitches over there!' The corpses have been brought from detention centres of the military branches. 'How am I going to carry that?' The conscript assigned to the hospital is afraid, he doesn't want to touch the emaciated remains, so he calls to his colleague, also a conscript. 'Go on, do it!' With frightened looks, the two young men are obliged to carry the corpses into the hangar.

Like a menacing presence, Bashar al-Assad watches over them. Up there, right above them. If the soldiers look up they can see the rocky slopes of Mount Mezzeh. On the summit, just 400 metres away as the crow flies, the fortress of Bashar al-Assad, surrounded by trees. The presidential palace, also called the Palace of the People, towers over the capital.

Behind its austere façade the huge presidential complex contains a multitude of living rooms, endless corridors, rooms with high ceilings covered in gilding. 'The entrance strangely resembles Hitler's Chancellery, but it has a more favourable position as it dominates the whole of Damascus', said the Lebanese Walid Jumblatt in *Syrie. Le Crépuscule des Assad* (*Syria: The Twilight of the Assads*), a documentary by Christophe Ayad and Vincent de Cointet broadcast on Arte in 2011. After years of isolation following the assassination of the Lebanese president Rafik Hariri, which many experts lay at the door of the Syrian intelligence services, Bashar al-Assad had become respectable again. In 2010, Walid Jumblatt, leader of the Druze community in Lebanon, made his way to Damascus. Having denounced the Syrian leader and his hold over Lebanon on many occasions, Jumblatt was now discovering his strange lair. Like a number of Western diplomats who resumed the dialogue with Assad.

At the foot of the presidential palace, then, every day, or almost, new dead bodies arrive, which the soldiers will learn to drag and carry then sort according to the branch of the intelligence services where they were detained. The same actions every day, or almost. The medical examiner arrives around 7 a.m. With a notebook in his hand, a block of large pages clipped together and divided into three columns, he moves from one corpse to the next. Each corpse bears two numbers, written in marker pen on the skin or on a strip of Scotch tape. The first is the prisoner number; the second, the branch of the intelligence services where he was detained. The medical examiner assigns a third one to him, for his medical report. Written on a card, this third number is placed on or next to the body. The photographer takes his pictures with a Nikon Coolpix P50 digital camera or a Fuji, then the doctor goes back to his notebook to note down the three numbers in the corresponding columns.

A soldier, acting as an 'eyewitness', accompanies him and gives him a description of the dead person to put in the first column: his approximate age, his build, skin and hair colour, any tattoos or bullet wounds … And the cause of death, which inevitably states: 'detainee died of cardiac arrest' or 'a respiratory problem'. Of course, there is no mention of torture anywhere on the form.

The medical examiner then draws a line under the information and passes on to the next person. On average, there are three or four dead people listed on each page. The medical report is archived in the offices of the medical examiners based at Tishreen hospital.

Once the photographs are finished, Caesar and his colleagues set off to the military police offices to draw up their own report, this one intended for military justice. Before the war, at the start of the Revolution, each corpse had its own record sheet. Gradually, as the corpses became more numerous, there was one sheet for every ten, then fifteen, twenty detainees.

These factsheets on headed paper from the department of criminal photography in the branch of the military police of the Syrian Arab Republic had pre-typed chapter headings: 'Judicial evidence', 'Photographic note of the incident', 'Details on the incident'.

The soldiers of the department of criminal photography, having marked 'deceased' on the form, have to fill in the form in pen.

An example from May 2013:[2]

Syrian Arab Republic
Military Police Branch
Judicial evidence
Department of Criminal Photography
Number XXX/XXX

Photographic note of the incident of death

Details of the incident:
We have been instructed by the general military prosecutor to photograph the incident of the death of detainees numbers XXXX/B, XXXX/B, XXXX/B, XXXX/B, XXXX/B, XXXX/B, XXXX/B, XXXX/B.

The detainees came from intelligence service branch 227.
The bodies were photographed in the morgue of military hospital 601 as requested on XX/XX/2013.
The photos were taken by Sergeant X.

Signed
Chargé d'affaires for judicial evidence, X
Major General, Parachute Regiment, Commander of Military Police, X

---

2   The document is reproduced in Appendix 1.

The photos of the corpses are then attached below. Then, finally, the stamp of general command of the army and the armed forces verifying the signatures and the photos.

The next day, another form, May 2013:

Syrian Arab Republic
Military Police Branch
Judicial evidence
Department of Criminal Photography
Number XXX/XXX
Photographic note of the incident of death

Details of the incident:
We have been instructed by the general military prosecutor to photograph the incident of the death of detainees numbers XXXX/B, XXXX/B, XXXX/B, XXXX/B, XXXX/B, XXXX/B, XXXX/B, XXXX/B, XXXX/B, XXXX/B, XXXX/B, XXXX/B, XXXX/B, XXXX/B, XXXX/B, XXXX/B, XXXX/B XXXX/B, XXXX/B,.

The detainees came from intelligence service branch 215. The bodies were photographed in the morgue of military hospital 601 as requested on XX/XX/2013.
The photos were taken by Sergeant X.

Signed
Chargé d'affaires for judicial evidence, X
Major General, Parachute Regiment, Commander of Military Police, X

4
The Archives of Death

Caesar

'It was even more painful for us to see the photos on the computer than it was to photograph the bodies. When we were there with the bodies we didn't have time to linger. The medical examiner was urging us on, the security service agents were watching us and noting our reactions. In Syria everyone is watching everyone else.

'As we weren't allowed to ask questions, it was easier just to take the photos without looking too closely at the wounds, simpler just not to feel anything.

'But in the silence of our office, we were freer, we had more time. And there, when we printed the photos and attached them, we couldn't avert our gaze. They were there in front of us. It was terrible. The picture was there. The detainee came back to life in front of us. We could really see the bodies, imagine the torture, feel the blows raining down. Then we had to write the report. As if to reinforce the memory of what we had seen. After a month in detention, the prisoners' faces could have changed completely. To the point where they were no longer recognizable.

'One of my friends died in detention. We photographed his body but didn't know who he was. It was only much later, when I was doing some discreet research for his father, that I realized that his photo had passed through our hands and that I hadn't recognized him. He had only been detained for two months. Yet he was someone I saw almost every day before his incarceration!

'His father found out from the military police that his son had died in detention. He didn't want to believe it. I told him: "I contacted the military hospital and they confirmed to me that your son is dead." In fact, I had searched through our archives and found the photo. Bound to secrecy, I couldn't tell him that, of course. No one knew that each body of a dead detainee was systematically photographed before being buried in a mass grave.

'In the beginning, we were disgusted. Nauseated. I could go almost three or four days without eating a thing. Then it became our daily routine, it became part of us. Asphyxiated. It was the only way we could get through it. What else could we do? If we expressed the way we felt, we could have been arrested and tortured to death and end up as one of those bodies. We were also afraid for our loved ones, afraid that they might be arrested and end up as one of those bodies too.

'One day, one of my colleagues was at the hospital in Mezzeh. The bodies were laid out next to each other. When he stood over one of them he got the impression the person was still alive. He was breathing softly. "Shall I photograph him? He's still alive", my colleague asked the soldiers in charge of moving the corpses.

'The medical examiner arrived. And he was angry: "What's this, he's still alive?! What am I supposed to do? It'll mess up all my numbers!" He was in a temper because he had already filled his notebook with the medical numbers of the corpses that he had given them one after the other. If this man was still alive, he would have to cross them all out, assign new numbers and write them all in again. "Don't worry, go and have a tea break and it'll all be sorted when you get back", one of the soldiers replied. When he got back, they finished the photos.

'My colleagues and I made up a team of a dozen photographers. We supported each other. But we couldn't really confide in each other. Sometimes you might whisper something with one of them, but you would keep the door open for fear that others might think you were plotting or criticizing the regime. In any case, we weren't allowed to close the door. We used to say: "On the Day of Judgement we will be asked to account for ourselves: 'What did you do during all those years with that criminal regime? Why did you not leave?'" And we felt afraid. What can you reply to that?

'We didn't know any more. We wondered: "But what's going on?"'

Tell the Story While There Is Still Time

Abu al-Leith, Mazen al-Hummada
'What's going on? We went onto the streets to protest against injustice and we became numbers, that's what's going on.' When Abu al-Leith talks, it is with a mixture of anger, bitterness and suffering. This former shopkeeper spent seven months in detention under the custody of Branch 227 of the military intelligence services, then in a cell in the civilian prison at Adra, nominally reserved for common-law criminals. A trust-worthy witness, then, whose long account leads us deep into the bowels of the detention centres.

On this afternoon in 2015, as the athletic looking Abu al-Leith walks briskly through the streets of Istanbul, passers-by would have no inkling of the hell that haunts this anonymous Syrian refugee.

But in the evening, invited to sit down in an out-of-the-way café, he shows what he has really become: a shadow of his former self, destroyed, an exile from his own body, lost in a world where he will 'never find peace' and has no idea where to go. Reassured somewhat by this discreet location, sitting on a cushion on the floor, at an hour of the day when confidences take time to emerge, Abu al-Leith gradually finds words that he had suppressed for many months. Yes, this former shopkeeper and opponent of the regime would like to return home to the mountains of Qalamoun, to the land where he was born and grew up, the land of his father and his father's father. But above all he wants to speak, has to speak.

Because in telling his own story he will express the suffering of all the opponents of the Assad regime. In presenting his own truth he will also become master of himself again. And it will mean that history is no longer written by the regime.

'At school, books and the Baath party inculcated bitterness, a hatred for democracy. Is it possible that a man can lead a country without his people? Do you have to be a dog to be worthy of more consideration? In the West, animals are treated better than we have been.'

On the morning of 17 December 2012 Abu al-Leith was sitting in his car on an isolated road, not far from Damascus. An army officer was about to desert and meet him there to join the ranks of the opposition. Using the excuse that he had to go out to buy something, the soldier would slip out of the barracks and come to find the activist. But his phone was tapped. When he rang to confirm his escape, it was agents from military intelligence who turned up, and they caught Abu al-Leith.

It was 9 a.m. They took him directly to the torture room at Branch 227 of military intelligence. Charged with the task of overseeing the suburbs of Damascus, Branch 227, nicknamed 'the branch of death', is housed in a building situated in the centre of the capital, a few hundred metres from the Sheraton hotel, which is frequented by tourists and business people. And less than 500 metres from the Damascus Opera, the jewel of the capital.

Before the interrogation had even started the investigators ordered him to undress, blindfolded him and struck his face with an iron cosh. 'There were two of them holding me by the arms', he told me. 'One of them was beating me round the head, the other on the shoulders and back. At one point I blacked out.'

'You are a terrorist', one of the interrogators said. They made him stand on a sort of crate, fastened his hands to the ceiling and then kicked the crate away. Hanging from his wrists, Abu al-Leith lost consciousness again. Three times. Each time he was 'woken up' with blows to the skull.

'If you own up to everything you'll be left in peace', these hellhounds advised him.

'I've got nothing to say', the activist replied.

Like his brothers, Abu al-Leith joined the Revolution very early on. In summer 2011, the peaceful Revolution began to become militarized. How could you go on marching in the streets chanting anti-regime slogans when army tanks occupied the squares, patrolled the neighbourhoods that had been hotspots of protest and encircled subjugated villages? How could you hold back when soldiers fired on protestors? Everywhere, civilians were arming themselves to protect the marches. At the same time, the number of deserters was increasing. A 'Free Syrian Army' was taking shape, combining local units of resistance under a single banner. The opposition believed it could bring down the regime by force.

Abu al-Leith's family came originally from Qalamoun. This mountainous, fiercely independent region has been in rebel hands since spring 2012. North of the capital, the region straddles the Damascus–Homs axis, a strategic route for the regime as it led to the littoral, which was considered a fiefdom of the Alawites, the community of President Bashar al-Assad. Abutting the Lebanese border, Qalamoun touches the southern extremity of the Bekaa valley, rear base for a large number of rebels, but also the fiefdom of Hezbollah, the Lebanese Shiite party, which supports the Syrian regime.

Abu al-Leith helped soldiers leave the ranks of the loyalist army. The man he was waiting for that morning in December 2012 confessed his 'activities' under torture. 'The men beating me wanted me to betray my accomplices too. They also gave me names and wanted me to say that they were terrorists. I was supposed to admit that I had taken part in demonstrations and denounce those who had organized them.'

Faced with his silence, his torturers ducked his head into a tub of water. 'I thought I was going to suffocate. When they took my head out, they gave me an electric shock, then stuck my head back under water.' After this, he was thrown on the floor of the toilets, half conscious, his face numb, unable to move for a long time, until he was finally taken before an officer, who sent him to a cell.

In this café in Istanbul he curls up a bit more on the cushions and takes another drag from the hookah. Silence. Unspeakable memories, images that are too present, the survivor forgets his listeners, then continues with an awkward smile: 'Being beaten was nothing compared with what happened to me after that. When you are beaten, you don't know what you are supposed to say. The intelligence services often already have information on you. They are trying to break you physically.

Especially when you aid the Free Syrian Army. But torture goes further. The system wants to destroy your humanity. We knew this was a criminal regime, but ... Bashar al-Assad wants to kill his people, not only by eliminating them physically, he wants to dehumanize them.'

After three days of abuse, Abu al-Leith was sent to a tiny box room where he could hardly move. He felt something next to him, reached out with his hand and felt a body. Then two or three, tangled together, cold. None was breathing, but there was a suffocating smell. There was something moving on his legs, scratching. Worms? The man began crying out, yelling, weeping. The corpses frightened him. He heard sounds outside, like screams of pain. He fell silent, listened, then in the end fell asleep in the middle of a pile of flesh. One or two days passed. An eternity. He realized that his jailers wanted him to identify the sounds coming through the walls. Wanted him to know that, very nearby, people were being tortured to death. At one point the cries grew louder, then stopped all of a sudden. And the torturer said three words: 'He is dead.' 'At that point', admitted the former detainee, 'I completely fell apart.'

A short while afterwards, his jailers came to get him and put him in another cell, a larger one. Naked and in the dark. There was another body there, still warm! The man had probably just uttered his last cry. Someone came to take him away, and Abu-al-Leith would remain alone in that room for nearly six months. Clearly, 'they' didn't want him to die. 'They' wanted to punish him, make him crack. Upstairs in the Branch 227 building the other cells were multiple-occupancy. Every day, the jailers did a roll call, reading out the name of the detainees, who had to reply 'Here'.

Abu al-Leith didn't have a name any more. He was not allowed to speak. From now on he was known as 'number 1'.

'Number 1!' the guards would shout out in the roll call. Abu al-Leith simply had to tap on his door in reply to show that he wasn't dead.

Solitude, silence, hunger, the cold of winter, then the heat of summer. Abu al-Leith began to have hallucinations. He asked God to finish him off. In the dark he heard someone murmuring to him, insisting: 'You mustn't die.' He even felt a comforting hand on his forehead. 'Put your hand there again', he asked. The shade did so and advised him to look after himself, to exercise to keep himself fit. 'But what do you want?' he said finally, raising his voice. 'Who are you talking to, dog?' called out one of the jailers. Abu al-Leith fell silent, realizing that he was losing his mind. 'But that voice helped me to hold on', he tells us today.

Another one, a real one this time, sustained him later. Abu al-Leith's isolated cell opened onto the corridor and the toilets. When he was allowed to go, he walked past others who had to lower their heads, not speak to him. And they weren't allowed to open the little shutter on his door to have a look at this prisoner number 1. One morning a man dared to ask him where he came from. Abu al-Leith hesitated.

'I'm from Baniyas', the man persisted. 'My name is Adel. Here is my phone number: XXX XXX. Will you ring my mother if you get out?'

Abu al-Leith took the risk: 'I'm from Qalamoun.'

'Don't go to sleep, don't talk, until I give three knocks.'

Later the man would slip him a piece of bread through the opening. 'He changed my life, he was really nice to me. Not like the other *soukhra*', Abu al-Leith says accusingly. For Adel was a *soukhra*, the Arabic term for 'forced labourer'.

Become a *Soukhra* or Die

The *soukhra* has become an essential cog in the death machine. In 2012, the cells of the intelligence services began to fill up. Since the start of the Revolution, and the multiplication of arbitrary arrests, prisoners had been arriving from every corner of the land. Before being sent to these detention centres, they were often kept in public buildings that had been secretly converted, both in the capital and in the provinces – houses, schools, stadiums, Baath party offices – where they sometimes stayed for weeks.

They even had to reopen the terrible prison at Palmyra, a concentration camp in the eastern desert. It is there over the course of thirty years that tens of thousands of political opponents, real or imagined – communists, Islamists, human rights activists – were locked up, sometimes in secret, tortured and executed. It fell into dilapidation and was closed in 2001, but was brought back into service ten years later, in June 2011. Three and a half months after the start of the Revolution. Mindful of the tyranny of the Assads, the jihadists of Islamic State destroyed the prison a few days after they conquered the town in April 2015. And with it, documents and other evidence of this hell on earth. A godsend for the regime.

In Damascus and in the provinces, there weren't enough jailers to deal with this influx of prisoners in the detention centres. So they had to rely on *shawish* and *soukhra*, introducing a new hierarchy of fear in the darkness of the cells. The *shawish* (Arabic for 'sergeants') were common-law prisoners who had been incarcerated for several years. Chosen by the administration, they managed the dormitories and kept an eye on – and punished – the prisoners. Following their orders, the *soukhra*, who were sometimes former criminals but more often civilians arrested during the Revolution, contributed to the maintenance of order. A chore done in return for a few favours or an extra helping of food. A privilege that would create conflict with other detainees.

Mazen al-Hummada was also a *soukhra*. It probably saved his life. Or maybe it was his fierce determination to get out alive to bear witness. Which is what he is doing today.

A technician with Schlumberger Ltd, a multinational oil company founded in France, he was working at the time in Deir ez-Zor in the northeast of the country. Having already been arrested twice, at the age of thirty-four, in April then in December 2011, for having filmed and posted online videos of demonstrations, this political opponent was called in a third time in spring 2012. On this occasion, having travelled to Damascus for a work meeting, he took the opportunity to deliver some milk to a female doctor who lived in a town on the outskirts that was being besieged by the regime. They had arranged to meet in a café in the covered souk of Hamidiye. No sooner had the doctor left than the activist and two of his nephews who were accompanying him were arrested and taken to a branch of the Air Force intelligence services.

He would spend eighteen months in detention, first of all in one of the many rooms at the military airport that had been transformed into cells, then two months in the Adra civilian prison and finally ten days at Political Security, before being released in September 2013.

After the first sessions of interrogation and torture, Mazen was thrown into a dormitory eleven metres long by six metres wide. He had to share this space with 180 others, all dressed like him in nothing but shorts or underpants. He never heard any mention of *soukhra*. In the cell, one of them supervised the twice-daily trips to the toilets, lining up the detainees in groups of ten and leading them off in single file so that they could relieve themselves two at a time. Another one was responsible for the medication. A handful of painkillers chucked in the bottom of one of the plastic bags that are used to sell Syrian flatbread, which he would distribute parsimoniously according to how seriously each person was injured.

'The pills were there just so that the jailers could tell their superiors that they had the means to take care of us', Mazen explains. 'It was a farce. The officers came to check that everything was in order and that correct procedure was being followed, but they knew perfectly well that there weren't enough to go round.'

'Do you have everything you need?' A lieutenant passes by in the corridor, giving the cells a cursory inspection.

'No! There isn't enough medicine. I'm ill!' one detainee dares to shout out from inside the dormitory. The man had had his toes cut off and had gangrene all the way up his leg.

'Yes. Yes, they have everything that they need', the jailer assures him.

'That's fine.' And the lieutenant leaves.

Once the officer has departed, the jailer sticks his foot in the door opening, livid.

'Who said there wasn't enough medicine?'

'Me', answers the injured man.

The guard drags him outside and with the help of two colleagues beats him with a plastic tube. Then they grab him by the lower part of his face, push it into the small gap at the top of the door and smash it until his teeth break.

Inside the cell, an army deserter tries to protest: 'He was just asking for something to treat his wounds.' 'Shut the fuck up', growls a jailer as he swings a stick around in the crowd of detainees.

Like all the others, Mazen lowers his eyes and grits his teeth. He braces himself, head sunk into his shoulders. He knows exactly what is coming next because he experienced it just a month earlier in another cell. A man, driven mad by the heat and promiscuity, had stood up, clambered over his comrades and hammered on the door: 'Why do you arrest us? You sons of bitches! Curses on Bashar, curses on Abu Bashar, curses on Hafez, curses on Abu Hafez, curses on Jamil Hassan!'[1]

The jailers had made everyone stand face to the wall and had beaten them, even those who fell to the ground, half dead. Then they had grabbed the 'insubordinate' and suspended him from the ceiling in the corridor outside the cell, hands bound behind his back, and had swung him back and forth.

Crack, crack, crack … 'I can still hear the sound of his shoulders being dislocated as they swung him.' After that, Mazen had kept a tight lip, no matter what went on in the cell.

Then one day he became a *soukhra*. His name had been put forward to the jailers by the *shawish*. Without a word to him. 'Tomorrow you will be a *soukhra*', the jailer told him.

A stroke of luck? At the time, Mazen was hopeful. He had been involved in clandestine militancy with opposition forces for years and had taken an active part in the Revolution. He was aware of the risks. 'I knew that I would be left to rot in here for a long time', he explains. 'I knew the only way to get out eventually was to be freed in a prisoner exchange. By being a *soukhra*, I would be able to get out of the cell, breathe fresh air.'

But already by the following day, reality had caught up with him. A man from the suburbs of Damascus had been transferred to their cell, his head dangling, his eyes

---

1   Jamil Hassan, head of Air Force Intelligence.

puffed up with the blows. The detainees laid him down on the rostrum at the back of the room, which was formerly a classroom. He survived for two days. He was the first body that Mazen had to take outside in his role as *soukhra*. He wrapped him in a blanket and, with the help of a teenage boy, carried him to the officers' room at the end of the corridor.

Then he came back. And broke down. He wanted to hurl himself against the door, swear at the guards, scream. His friends held him back, he was crying. One of his nephews with whom he had been arrested and who was still with him, a man made of stern stuff, took hold of his hands, held him together: 'Be careful. If you do that, they will torture you to death.' Then he led him to the toilets and threw some water on his face. Mazen would remain in a daze for hours before he pulled himself together.

'I had forgotten my brothers' advice', this survivor now admits. Mazen is the youngest in a family of eleven brothers and eight sisters, born of two different mothers. His brothers had often mentioned prison. The older ones had experienced years of detention. In the evening, at home or in meetings with other opponents, they talked about it, and the young Mazen listened. 'When you're locked up you have to forget about the outside world', they would say. 'Otherwise you're lost. You have to think only about the place you're in, look at the walls, count the number of tiles, concentrate on what you're eating. If you let the outside world into your cell, you will die ...'

Being a *Soukhra* is also a Form of Torture

The second body that Mazen had to take out of the dormitory was that of a soft-spoken young man with a nice singing voice. Saleh. Outside, the loyalist army was battling the rebels in the town of Mouadamiye.

Situated next to the southern airport, the town had been surrounded by regime troops for months. Now the fighting was coming close to the airfields and the buildings that had been transformed into prisons. The airport officers had cut off the electricity to extinguish all the lights and make the place less of a target for the insurgents' guns.

In the dormitory, the blades of the ventilator had stopped. It very quickly became airless. After a few hours, Saleh had gone up to the door and shouted. 'Who's that animal banging on the door?' a guard had asked. Saleh had asked for air. The jailers had grabbed him, beaten him and brought him back.

When he died, there was pandemonium in the room. The jailers had to come in five or six at a time to push people apart with baton blows, to let Mazen and another *soukhra* take Saleh's body out to place it in a military ambulance. Usually, when one of them died, the whole cell gathered, hands over their eyes, heads lowered, holding back the tears. A cleric would recite a few verses of the Quran in a lowered voice.

Virtually every day, one of the detainees died of suffocation. Mostly one of the old or infirm. The only breath of air inside the cell came through the gap under the door. Those nearest to it were reluctant to give up their spot. It was mainly officers who had deserted who sat here. When someone at the back was suffocating, it was only after some insistence that he was allowed a space to sit near the draught of air.

'We were all pressed together', Mazen recalls. 'You wouldn't put 150 sheep into a shed designed for 50. But there were 180 of us packed in there! We were so starved we'd have fought each other. Hunger destroys all morality. Hunger has no religion, it is atheist.'

Mazen stole. A morsel of bread, a spoonful of rice, of soup.

Around midday the jailers would summon him and three other *soukhra* to unload the lorries filled with canteens of rice, sacks of bread and crates of tomatoes. They took the food to near the officers' room and then divided it up between the cells. Mazen pinched some when soldiers' backs were turned. At the start of his detention, the meals were almost sufficient. Little by little, with the confrontations in the capital and the increase in the price of foodstuffs, the stewpots became half empty, and on top of that the officers started appropriating some of the supplies to sell on.

Breakfast was kept in the cell: bread and labneh, a thick, salty white cheese, in black and white plastic containers, placed on a shelf above the toilets. Lunch, stripped to the bare minimum, was distributed in the cell. As for dinner, that was stocked in the tent. The *soukhra* went to fetch it in the evening.

A tent – which contained a resting area with three beds and a workspace with a desk – had been erected by the jailers in the courtyard in front of the prison buildings. The jailers had even made a small garden with plants in old tin cans and would come here to drink tea in peace.

In the morning, Mazen would be woken by the sound of the officers' boots as they arrived at work or the footsteps of the jailers taking up their shift of guard duty. It would be 6 or 7 a.m. '*Yellah*, boys, it's time to eat breakfast, on your feet, otherwise they will get angry and beat us. Come on, wake up.'

Later in the morning, the *soukhra* went out to clean the cells, the corridors and officers' rooms. Mazen went to the jailers' tent to slip on some flip-flops and, with a bucket of Lodaline and a cheap mop, he cleaned the floors. A squeegee for wiping off the dirty water and clothes for wiping. 'These were T-shirts and trousers belonging to the detainees', Mazen explains. 'The investigators made us undress before being interrogated and tortured. Then we went to the cells in our underpants. When I was arrested I had just been to a work meeting and was dressed smartly in a Stefanel shirt, jeans and black Italian shoes. Clothes like that were confiscated by the soldiers; the other, poorer-quality stuff was thrown into a room and given to us to wipe the floor with.'

There was often a jailer behind his back who would try to speed him up and mistreat him if his pace dropped. His back bent over, Mazen endured in silence and made a mental note of everything that happened around him. He memorized the names of the officers and the torturers. He observed scenes where detainees were blindfolded. He calculated the length of the corridors, the area of the cells. His aim? To remember. He would be free one day. He would tell his story.

And so, over several evenings in that spring of 2015, the former prisoner did tell his story, with passion, in an uninterrupted, confused stream of words. He revealed names, described places, gave details of events, visited the pain all over again. The only thing missing was exact dates. However, the detainees did mark a calendar on the wall using an olive stone. Every day they moved the marker, made out of a gummed label from a sack of bread. This survivor remembered, but his thoughts sometimes zigzagged. When he couldn't remember a name, he got agitated and immediately phoned a former cellmate, like him a refugee in Europe. 'Do you remember so and so? What was his name again?' He had a good memory before the Revolution and his imprisonment. It remained strong during the first months of his detention, but since his liberation it has let him down at times.

One day he managed to swing a telephone call with the *shawish*. The latter had brought in a jailer's mobile in a box of salt. In exchange for some money paid by an opponent friend on the outside, Mazen was able to let his family know that he was being held by Air Force intelligence. And also give them the names of seventy other detainees, so that their families could be informed too. He was denounced to another jailer by a jealous fellow prisoner, who accused him of having telephoned rebels with the Free Syrian Army, and was placed in solitary confinement in a box room for several days.

Every week, when Mazen cleaned the office of special missions at the military airport, he saw detainees being led in single file, eyes blindfolded, wrists handcuffed behind their backs. They were being disembarked from planes that had flown in from Hama, Homs, sometimes Aleppo, the great city of the north, divided in two by the forces of regime and those of the opposition.

When a man was arrested in the provinces he was questioned initially in a local detention centre. A report on his interrogation was then sent to the central office in Damascus, which decided, based on the importance of the individual and the information they might possess, whether or not to send him to the capital.

Often prisoners could not be transferred directly. This was a country at war: travel was difficult and cells in some locations were full up. Sometimes detainees had to wait weeks in improvised jails until the already overcrowded intelligence branches in Damascus emptied out a bit. The trajectories of certain prisoners resembled a spider's web, from one point to the next, with no rational explanation.

Transfer of Corpses

Amer al-Homsi
Sometimes, even the bodies of detainees who had died in the provinces were sent to the capital. Doctor Amer al-Homsi had been practising for fifteen years at the

government hospital in Homs. In 2011 and 2012, before fleeing overseas, he saw corpses picked up by the authorities to be transported by helicopter to the military hospital in town or directly to Damascus. Nicknamed the 'capital of the Revolution', Homs paid one of the heaviest tolls in this war. The regime really went after the country's third city, which is situated at a strategic crossroads between Damascus and the north towards Aleppo and Turkey and the Alawite fiefdom and the Mediterranean to the east. Widespread arrests, intensive bombardment of certain neighbourhoods, such as Bab Amro in February 2012, a rebel bastion that was literally crushed when it was recaptured in March.

'Our hospital became a detention centre, a sort of barracks', the doctor recalls from his current refuge in a neighbouring country. 'Every day, dozens of detainees, whether injured or not, were brought here, tied to the beds, blindfolded, beaten, given electric shocks. At one point, there were several hundred of them on all floors. We weren't allowed to speak to them. When they got out of the lorries, we shut ourselves inside for fear we might recognize one of them.' One of the first injured detainees that Amer al-Homsi had to treat, in spring 2011, was a young demonstrator. When he arrived, he had deep cuts round his ankles where he had been chained. He died after three days of beatings. When his body was returned to his family, his eye sockets were empty ... Other bodies were returned to their families crudely sewn up, as if they had been harvested for organs. The parents then had to sign a piece of paper saying that their child had been killed by 'terrorists'. Gradually, the security services started demanding money from families in return for their child's remains. Many didn't have the means; others did, but didn't turn up out of fear of being arrested in turn.

In the morgue that was set up in the basement, the smell soon became overpowering. Especially in January and March 2012, when the regime's repression of rebel neighbourhoods intensified. 'The fridges were full, the bodies piled up on the floor, we had to work with our mouths and noses covered', Amer al-Homsi explains. Most of the corpses were taken away in small lorries to be buried in the cemeteries of the surrounding villages. But a few were sent to Damascus. 'I'm sure it was to show to the heads of the security branches that these men had indeed been arrested and were now dead.'

I Was No Longer a Human Being

Abu al-Leith
Abu al-Leith, the man from Qalamoun, was still alive when he was brought before a tribunal. He was taken by military police in charge of the transfer of detainees.

After six months in the detention centre Abu al-Leith was taken out of his cell and led away blindfolded in a minibus to a place he didn't know. In an office, someone asked for his name.

'I am number 1.'

He received a blow for that.

'What are you called?'

So he gave his real name and was told: 'You and your family are all terrorists.' The man grabbed his hand and took his fingerprints. He was stuffed inside a car with some others, head down for the whole journey. At army roadblocks the soldiers wanted to 'beat this terrorist' with their rifle butts. They arrived at the military tribunal at Mezzeh, southwest of the capital. When they removed his blindfold, Abu al-Leith nearly passed out. It had been months since his eyes had been exposed to this much sunlight. By his side, he saw one of the former officers whom he had tried to help desert. As well as other poor wretches, naked, with stinking wounds and infected legs. Some had scabies. Abu al-Leith was frightened by these grey, soulless faces. He scratched himself and his uncut fingernails broke his skin.

The judge accused him of 'bankrolling an armed gang', 'abetting the defection of officers' and 'collaboration with foreign forces'. He was sent to Adra civilian prison. On the way there, he spent a night in a military branch, in an overcrowded room where the ceiling was too low to stand upright. They threw rice on the ground for them. He didn't manage to get anything to eat. When they arrived at the prison, there were a hundred or so men standing in the yard. The sun was burning their wounds. They were promised food, clothing and a visit from a doctor. They formed a queue to go into a room where they got their hair cut and their nails clipped. Inside, there were four or five mirrors standing against the wall. 'Why are you looking at me?' Abu al-Leith said tetchily. In the mirror he could see a man observing him. Disfigured face, emaciated body. Abu al-Leith was about to challenge him again when he realized that the reflection was him. 'I wasn't a human being any more, I wanted revenge.'

With his head shaved, the thin stream of water with which he could wash himself pierced his skin like nails.

In prison, he didn't speak, or rather only to argue or fight with other detainees. In the huge dormitory where they had all been left to rot, a life prisoner, who had been incarcerated for fifteen years, had set himself up in a corner with a television. At Adra, everything had a price, visits as well as the possibility of receiving books or other goods.

The lifer was strong and sturdy, and he also came from the mountains of Qalamoun. He took Abu al-Leith under his wing, domesticated him, fed him like a child. Lent him his mobile, which he had smuggled in. His phone call home was indescribable: crying and wailing. 'They couldn't believe it was really me. They were convinced that I was dead. My mother fainted.'

Abu al-Leith's brothers knew an officer of the regime. They bought an amnesty for him and promised to release some prisoners from the loyalist forces. On the homeward journey they were able to pass regime roadblocks thanks to this officer and roadblocks of the Free Syrian Army thanks to his brothers. When our survivor stepped out in front of the family home, his mother was there along with his four sisters and four of his five brothers. Cousins and neighbours too. Abu al-Leith reeled a bit at the clamorous welcome. Too much noise, too many people. The eldest brother intervened: 'Let him be, he needs some peace and quiet.' The former detainee went upstairs to his room; a doctor gave him a sedative and a sleeping pill. Abu al-Leith remained sequestered there for a week before he was able to talk to anyone. And begin to find some semblance of normal life.

In the hills Hezbollah, the Lebanese Shiite party supported by Iran, which had come to the assistance of the regime, had sent its men to fight the rebels of the Free Syrian Army. There was a series of battle. Abu al-Leith kicked his heels in the family home while two of his brothers were bearing arms with the FSA. By walkie-talkie he told the eldest one: 'If you go off to fight, I will go too.' But he knew he wasn't capable of it. Just as he wasn't capable of telling his family what he had lived through in the previous seven months. The eldest brother commanded a battalion and led a victorious assault against the Lebanese forces; the other one fought by his side. The latter would die a short while later in another offensive.

At home, Abu al-Leith's mother never left him. After the death of her son on the battlefield, she had just learned that another had died in a military intelligence detention centre. Two of her five sons were dead. This grim death toll had to end. Especially as a third son was also in the hands of the intelligence services. Abu al-Leith had to leave the country and seek refuge abroad. To carry on the name of his family.

He left Syria feeling that he was a traitor.

5

Communities and Religions

Caesar

'At the very beginning, my colleagues and I had discussions. Most of them were critical of the demonstrators: "We had security before. Why are these groups of hooligans and their foreign backers trying to cause problems? They are destabilizing the regime. We were fine before that, we could leave our cars unlocked, there was no theft, our wives could walk the streets at any hour of the day or night. Look how it is now!"

'My colleagues believed that what was happening was nothing to do with them, that it was far away. But when the soldiers went home on leave to their villages, they started to see the army killing civilians, soldiers raping women and girls, burning down houses, crushing cars under their tanks. They realized that sectarian and religious hatred was on the increase and that it was becoming impossible to negotiate with the regime.

'In the large sectors of the army the soldiers sleep in dormitories. In the smaller sectors, or in services like mine, they spend the night in their offices. Before the events, the soldiers preferred to sleep alone to have some peace. Afterwards, little by little, they wanted to sleep in groups. Like chickens huddling together to keep warm and stick together out of fear of the fox. We didn't know where the trouble would come from. The regime? The rebels?

'Originally there were two beds in each of our offices. Then we started carting the beds from one room to another. One soldier brought his, then another, then another. As it happens, we organized ourselves according to our natural affinities, with guys from the same village or region, or of the same religious confession: Druzes with Druzes, Alawites with Alawites, Sunnis with Sunnis.

'We needed to stick together because we were afraid of being accused of things we hadn't done. Before the Revolution we were not particularly aware of differences between us. But little by little people wanted to start settling scores. Malicious gossip became widespread. Everyone might believe what other people were saying about such-and-such a person. Lots of soldiers were arrested by the security services over the course of four or five months on trumped-up accusations. Sometimes they were accused of just "thinking about deserting". Soon there were informants in all the services.

'In each military sector, one officer is responsible for security. Often he is an Alawite. He conducts an inquest and receives complaints before sending them to the intelligence services, bypassing normal judicial procedure.

'For example, it is forbidden to pray during normal service hours. Before, when a soldier went ahead and did it, he got a simple warning without the matter being passed on to the intelligence services. With the Revolution, an accusation of praying has become a reason to make a complaint against someone. This has become more serious with the passage of time, because the regime started to lump revolutionaries together with terrorists. It's true that, at the start, the revolutionaries came primarily from largely poor, conservative Sunni regions. But this has got nothing to do with terrorism. For the regime, praying five times a day means that you are a Muslim Brother, whereas the majority of Sunnis do it as part of their duty towards God and don't have anything to do with the Muslim Brotherhood.

'Hafez al-Assad, the father of Bashar, killed thousands of Muslim Brothers in the 1980s, claiming that they were terrorists. His son makes the same false association between demonstrators, Muslim Brothers and terrorists.

'The majority of conscripts and soldiers in the military police are Sunnis, the officers are Alawites. Before the Revolution we all knew which village people came from, what religious confession they belonged to, but it wasn't important. We were one big family. We avoided conflict.

'In the army, the Alawites spoke with a Damascus accent. After the early months of the Revolution they started exaggerating their dialect, pronouncing *qaf*[1] more emphatically, for example. It was a way of provoking us and showing that they were proud to be with the regime. Even the Sunnis who supported Bashar al-Assad started affecting an Alawite accent. They did so even more when they thought that the regime was close to victory, to show that they were on the winning side.

'Like many others, I was permanently under scrutiny. All my actions, my gestures were noted; even my feelings, the way I looked at things, were analysed.

'Relations between the soldiers and their officers became tense. Our televisions, which only broadcast Syrian state TV channels, were confiscated. We could

---

1 The letter q.

only watch the one in the canteen. Mobile phones were also banned. I hid mine in my sock. Landlines were tapped. When soldiers rang their families they always said that everything was fine. The families couldn't say anything about the situation back in their village.

'Sometimes, friends who had deserted to join the Free Syrian Army phoned me at home. I hung up straight away. I was so afraid to speak to them because you could be arrested for "communicating with a terrorist group". Afterwards, I wouldn't be able to sleep. The next day at the office, I'd be very worried.

'Increasingly, the soldiers and the Sunni conscripts began to desert. Every week, several would run away from the military police. At the start, they would go on leave and not return, but instead stay with their families. Then leave was rationed and finally abolished for conscripts, because the regime feared more desertions. Some soldiers took advantage of family funerals to run away. So then the regime restricted permissions to attend funerals.

'Some soldiers pretended to be mad to try to get a discharge. Some broke their own arm to get a medical certificate in order to return home. But it was becoming more and more dangerous to desert. Soldiers almost never served in the region they came from. Conscripts or those in training were sent to the other end of the country. That caused problems. At the start of the Revolution, the roads were reliable, the regime controlled the territory. Gradually, the rebels began to conquer and control certain zones. Soldiers couldn't travel around easily.

'Because of desertions and a drop-off in recruitment, Sunnis became less and less numerous in the army and in our service. They were replaced with Alawites.

'Whatever the army service, you could only confide in a handful of people. When a colleague wanted to desert he couldn't tell us, of course, but he made himself understood through his way of talking to us, getting close to us, looking at us more affectionately, being nicer. He was saying goodbye in an indirect manner. It was a way of saying: "Forgive me if I desert." Sometimes he seemed distracted, his mind seemed elsewhere. And you could see the fear in his face.

'It was hard when we had worked together for a long time. We wondered: "Will he succeed? Will he die? And what about us, will we die?" I too wanted to run away, but I couldn't. I had made a commitment. I had to finish what I had started. Copying all these photos and hiding them somewhere safe.'

Competition, Rivalry and Jealousy

Munir Abu Muaz, Mazen al-Hummada
The Syrian army, 300,000 strong in 2011, was one of the mainstays propping up the regime. It was the army that had put Hafez al-Assad in power in a coup d'état in November 1970. To ensure its loyalty, Hafez al-Assad appointed members of his clan and members of his religious confession, the minority Alawites, in key positions.

The Alawite Bashar al-Assad continues this policy of allegiance instituted by his father, systematically favouring members of his own community. The higher echelons and army commanders are 85–90 per cent of the Alawite confession. A few are Christian or Sunni. The rank and file are predominantly Sunni.

Faced with a Sunni majority, Assad father and son both exploited fear of minorities, Alawite and Christian, to get them on board. Offering themselves as a (false) secular bulwark, they were able to play the religion card, appealing to both community and financial interests.

In April 2011, Bashar al-Assad gave the illusion that he was listening to the protestors. He brought the forty-eight-year state of emergency to an end, but at the same time authorized the police to transfer powers of arrest and detention to the security and intelligence services.

And, to ratchet up the repression, the leadership formed a Central Management Crisis Cell, made up of the commanders of the armed forces, the Defence and Interior Ministries and the heads of the intelligence services. This committee produced daily reports on the situation across the whole country. With the support of President Assad, it took decisions and sent its orders to the Office of National Security, the key organ of repression in the country thanks to its local 'emergency committees' – more so than the army itself.

The military could not guarantee the stability of the regime without the multiple intelligence services and the local Baath party offices. In the first months of the Revolution, when the army attacked the rebel neighbourhoods that were protesting, the intelligence agents prevented the activists from organizing, arrested them, tortured them and killed them. In August 2011, a 'highly confidential' note was faxed from the Office of National Security to the heads of local emergency committees. An extract: 'Following a decision by the Central Management Crisis Cell, the Office of National Security asks all heads of security committees to launch a daily campaign [...] to apprehend the persons who are implicated in fomenting the demonstrations, those who are financing the demonstrations, those who are organizing the demonstrations, the co-conspirators who are in communication with persons living abroad in order to garner support of the demonstrations and those who are tarnishing the image of Syria in the foreign media and international organizations.'

This document was recovered in Syria by the Commission for International Justice and Accountability (CIJA). Under the direction of former international lawyers, this organization works with Syrian civilians who collect evidence of war crimes and crimes against humanity to create files to be used at some future legal tribunal.

After this confidential note of August 2011, hundreds of names of persons to be arrested were transmitted by the army, as shown in this document from 2012, also discovered by the CIJA. On the original[2] there were crosses marked against five of the six names. These crosses indicate that the person had already been arrested, or that they were dead or that they were no longer in Syria ... The two holes on the right-hand side of this document showed that it had been in a loose-leaf folder.

Urgent telegram

5th Division
Number: XXX
Date: XXX

To the commanders of the following brigades: */12-15-112-132 and of the regiment 175/*

To the commanders of the following battalions: */56-58-59-60-127/*

Re: letter number XXX, delivered on XXX by Branch 265 of the intelligence services of the command of the security group at Deraa and seen by the 1st Troop Corps.
We request that you add the following names to the list of wanted persons, that you arrest them immediately once

2   See Appendix 2.

located and bring them to relevant security agencies. The names are:

XXX XXX
XXX XXX
XXX XXX
XXX XXX
XXX XXX
XXX XXX

Signed by the command of the 5th Division

Notes:
This copy for brigade, regiment and battalion commanders only. It should not be distributed or disseminated.
*The brigade, regiment and battalion commanders should transmit only the names of the wanted persons to units under their command. The names should be communicated **only** to relevant personnel at roadblocks.*

The intelligence services, known as the Mukhabarat by the Syrians, are divided into four sections: Military Security (the most important), General Security (general intelligence), Political Security (attached to the Interior Ministry) and Air Force Security (created by Hafez al-Assad, a former pilot). These services in turn are subdivided into central branches in Damascus, regional branches in the provinces and local branches in towns throughout the country. Each branch has one or more detention centre, large or small.

'An archipelago of torture centers', according to Human Rights Watch in its report of July 2012: 'Torture Archipelago: Arbitrary Arrests, Torture, and Enforced Disappearances in Syria's Underground Prisons since March 2011'.[3] The NGO's argument is supported by

---

3 http://www.hrw.org/reports/2012/07/03/torture-archipelago.

witness statements, maps locating the detention centres and sketches demonstrating the overcrowding of cells. Those in charge of the branches of the intelligence services are also identified.

On the ground, the intelligence chiefs all hated each other. In early March 2015, the bodyguards of Rafik Chehade, the head of Military Security, are said to have beaten up Rustom Ghazaleh, the chief of Political Security. Both men were dismissed on the spot by Bashar al-Assad.

The two men had loathed each other for ages. Power rivalries and the division of profits from contraband both played a part. The Sunni general Rustom Ghazaleh had become a troublesome witness in the international inquest into the assassination in Beirut in 2005 of the Lebanese prime minister Rafik Hariri, an assassination widely attributed to the Syrian secret services. Ghazaleh did not long survive the beating: he was dead within a few weeks.

The competition between intelligences services was rampant even in the corridors of the detention centres. In two years of imprisonment, the engineer Munir Abu Muaz was transferred between four branches of two security services and spent six months in the terrible Saydnaya prison, about thirty kilometres from Damascus, a jail reserved for political detainees and Islamists, a worthy successor to the prison at Palmyra.[4]

Two years of detention in the terrible world of the cells during which Munir had to constantly adapt to new forms of brutality, the turnover of his jailers matching that of their superiors in the detention centres and in the security services themselves.

---

4 In August 2016, Amnesty International denounced the daily hell of Saydnaya prison in an original and impressive interactive webpage at: https://saydnaya.amnesty.org.

Munir Abu Muaz was arrested for the first time on 16 March 2011, in the very early days of the Revolution, by Political Security, which was charged with keeping an eye on the activities of political opponents. Along with a few other activists, this IT technician and political opponent had organized a sit-in in front of the Ministry of the Interior. Munir would spend a week in a cell of Political Security. 'I wasn't tortured much', he recounts. 'Just beaten, alone in a cell. At that time it wasn't one of the more fierce branches.'

He was arrested a second time in March 2012 as he was about to leave the country to attend an opposition meeting in Istanbul. Just as he was crossing the Syrian–Lebanese border with his wife, the police pulled him over and made arrangements to transfer him to a detention centre.

'Where are you taking him?' his wife asked.

'We're taking him away for a day or two, then we'll send him back to you', a policeman said.

'Two days. We all know what that means with your sort. He won't be coming back', his wife cried.

'That's no concern of yours.'

She wouldn't see him again for another two years. He had lost eighty kilograms and was unrecognizable. On the photo taken on his release he is smiling, but you have to look carefully at the distinguishing marks on his face to recognize the man who is now telling his story in spring 2015.

Munir was sent, blindfolded, hands tied, to Branch 215 of Military Security, behind the Carlton Hotel in the Kfar Sousa quarter of Damascus. It is a seven- or eight-storey building which formerly belonged to the electric company. There, they confiscated all his belongings: computer, watch, identity card.

Then he was stripped, beaten.

'Why were you going to Lebanon?' asked one of his interrogators.

'A holiday.' Slaps and punches in the face.

'A holiday at this time of year? You are an organizer. People have given us your name. You organize demonstrations in the country.'

'That's not true.' Another slap.

'Give us the passwords for your Facebook and Skype accounts.'

Munir attempted to play for time in order to allow – as prearranged – one of his contacts in Russia to change the passwords of their group if he hadn't received news after a certain number of hours.

There followed a week in a cell two metres square shared with three other detainees. After several interrogation sessions, one of his torturers came and showed him a bundle of papers on which were printed all of his Skype conversations for the previous few weeks. Then he was transferred to Branch 291, the 'administrative' branch of Military Security. New interrogators. New beatings. Munir had to stay standing, his hands tied behind his back, his knees bent, his head against the wall. Without moving. He was beaten every time he fell.

A new cell. This time with a hundred others, stuffed into a room fifty metres square. Some bread and a few olives in the morning, rice and bread at midday, a tomato or soup in the evening. Then the servings of food got smaller and the number of detainees exploded. Munir tried to speak to the jailers.

'We need more food', he dared to say.

'What you are doing can be considered a rebellion against the state', the guard retorted.

'If you want to talk about laws, I can tell you that I have been here for three months without any of my family knowing of my whereabouts. I am isolated. I have no access to a lawyer. That is illegal.'

'You are being held here legally.'

'No, I'm not. I don't even know what I am accused of.'

'The judge extended your detention.'

'Which judge? I've never seen a judge!'

'If you persist, we can just kill you and throw you in a grave then say that you were shot by terrorists. No one will be any the wiser.'

In early May 2012, a soldier of about thirty, who was suspected of contacts with a deserter, came back after a two-day interrogation. He couldn't walk any more. Two prisoners would lift him up and carry him to the toilet, where he would urinate blood. 'His body was blackened. He smelled bad, as if something inside was rotting', Munir remembers. One detainee, a doctor, asked them to provide medical assistance, but his appeals fell on deaf ears. Two days later it was the *shawish* of the cell who knocked on the door.

'There's one here not moving', he shouted to the guards.

'When he's dead, bring him to me', a jailer replied.

'He's not moving at all', the *shawish* insisted.

The jailer opened the door and took the body away.

After three and a half months, Munir was sent to Branch 216 of military intelligence, the 'patrol branch'. There he was interrogated again. 'You didn't tell 215 anything. So we are starting again', an investigator warned him. 'We need something from you.'

Munir was sentenced by a special tribunal and transferred to Saydnaya prison, where he would stay six months before being sent on to another intelligence agency, as his name had been mentioned in connection with another case involving political activists. This time it was the terrible Air Force intelligence service that would be dealing with him.

Mezzeh, the Hospital of Death

Part of the Air Force Security network was based at the military airport of Mezzeh. Munir and twelve other detainees, dressed only in underpants, were locked up in a room less than nine metres square. No ventilation, no beds, just a faint glimmer of light coming through the boarded window. The food was rotten. Everyone had dysentery. The jailers opened the door twice a day to allow the detainees to go to the toilet at the end of the corridor. A short journey, during which they were beaten. They had to hurry as they only had a few minutes in total. No water, no hygiene. Those who lagged behind were thrashed. Many of them would return to the cell with their feet and legs spattered with excrement. The number of cases of dysentery increased. Sometimes, detainees had to relieve themselves in a corner of the cell. 'You are disgusting', the guards would shout at them. They were dirty, for sure. But basically they were ill. They used a bottle to urinate in between visits. On two occasions Munir soiled himself. Another time, a man couldn't hold it in, and the diarrhoea flowed out under the cell door. 'The jailer came and ordered the man to clean it up with his tongue', Munir recounts.

Munir grew weak with the dysentery. A doctor in the security branch agreed to send him to hospital. One evening, a jailer summoned him and five others. In the corridor outside the cells they threw them a stack of clothes that clearly belonged to other prisoners and had been piled up in a room. 'Get dressed!' Munir grabbed some trousers and a shirt. A jailer wrote a number on a piece of tape and stuck it on his forehead. 'That's your number for the hospital, you don't give your name there.'

The little group of prisoners arrived at the military hospital of Mezzeh, Hospital 601. They were led to the hospital services wing, which was separated by a road from the laboratories, where the 'grave garages' were, the ones where Caesar and his team photographed the numbered corpses.

Munir stayed there three months. Most of the time tied to the bed, sometimes with two or three others. As in the cells of the various branches, the toilet trips were regulated and infrequent. In an emergency, a *soukhra* would hand the patient one of the bags used to wrap bread in. Munir would inflate it to make sure it didn't leak, and afterwards hide it under his bed. A piece of the foam mattress would serve as toilet paper.

Every morning, around 7 or 8 o'clock, a *soukhra* and an officer would tour the dormitories. The doctor would only do rounds once every three or four days. The same greeting every day: 'Anyone died?'

Some nights, officers of the regime would beat a patient to death. Through the opaque glass of his room Munir could see the shapes, hear the noises, the muffled voices. The next morning the bedridden detainees would spread the word: 'There was an execution party.' Later, the *soukhra* would share his fears with Munir: 'They might kill me because I have witnessed the executions in the hospital.'

Another time, in a room in this large hospital establishment in Damascus, Mazen al-Hummada, the *soukhra* in the Air Force intelligence services who wanted so much to remember in order to tell his story later, participated in two executions himself. Yet he spent no more than four days in Mezzeh hospital. Shortly after these interrogation sessions, the activist urinated blood and had pains in his kidneys.

One morning, when he was in a cell at the military airport, he was told that he would be leaving for hospital. Along with the others, he was dressed only in underpants. A jailer handed him a bloodstained top that had been picked up from the clothing taken from detainees when they first arrived. Blindfolded, handcuffed, loaded onto an ambulance, he arrived at the hospital ten minutes later. When he got out of the ambulance, the nurses spitefully struck them on the back with their flip-flops, treating them like terrorists.

He was taken down to the basement of the building and shown into a room with all the other detainees of Air Force intelligence services. To the side was a room reserved for those of the military intelligence services.

In his room, there were about twenty sick men sharing ten beds, sitting side by side, their feet tied to the metal frames by iron or nylon chains.

A male nurse who was trying to insert a needle in his arm to administer some glucose serum managed to pierce a vein. At the sight of his blood he gave a cry, but the nurse threatened to beat him. Another *soukhra*, Ahmed, who worked at the hospital and with whom he had to share a bed, warned him: 'Don't ask for anything. Don't raise your hand. Don't say anything.' Mazen didn't understand, and didn't dare ask any questions, as the patients were not allowed to talk among themselves, but he recalled stories his cellmates had told, to which he had scarcely lent an ear: 'The male nurses beat us in the hospital.'

Killed them too. At night. A jailer opened the door of the room. He was drunk. 'Who needs medicine?' 'Me', a feeble voice replied. The jailer went over to him: 'The divine tribunal has condemned you to death', then hit him on the face with a plastic tube. And he struck him several times. The voice fell silent. The man then turned to the others: 'Listen, you pack of dogs, they call me Azrael.[5] My mission is take souls, to steal the souls of those whose life is nearing its end.'

---

5 The angel of death.

Mazen would witness Azrael come into their room on two occasions. Once the beating was over, Ahmed the *soukhra* opened the padlock which held the chain, took hold of the dead man's foot, pulled his body to the ground and dragged it to the toilets.

'The first time I needed to go to the toilet', Mazen recounts, 'I came across three bodies that were half blue, piled one on top of the other. The smell was terrible. They must have been there for days.' Mazen pushed the door shut, opened the one next to it. There were two other corpses, apparently recently dead. Ahmed explained that the dead bodies are piled up here until they can be removed – every two or three days.

On the fourth day, Mazen begged the doctor to get him out of there. 'You're not well yet', the doctor replied. 'I'm much better, I want to return to my cell.' Anywhere was better than this place of death.

Just a few minutes away in that same residential quarter life went on as normal. Heedless, deaf and blind to what was going on the other side of the wall.

Another World

One morning in October 2013, the classroom at the Lycée Français Charles-de-Gaulle in Damascus was filled with sunlight. Among the students, a teenage girl with long dark curls smiled at the camera and, speaking with a charming slight hint of an accent, replied in French to the journalist from Agence France-Presse: 'At first it was difficult to work with the situation outside the *lycée*, but we got used to it. When we come to school it is like another world. We are here, learning. We study, we are together. We are all right.'

After March 2012, and the closure of the French embassy in Syria by Nicolas Sarkozy in protest against the repressive regime, all French institutions left the country. At the *lycée* and at the French school, both built in Mezzeh, the quarter at the foot of the presidential palace, the teachers who defied this decision continued to take in Franco-Syrian or Francophone students from families close to, or members of, the regime. In peacetime, there had been more than 900 primary and secondary schoolchildren; now there were 200, most of whom were accompanied by bodyguards. In some classrooms the regime's flag – three bands (red, white and black) and two stars – hung on the wall.

Built on an enclosed site on former desert terrain, the small white buildings of the French school are spread over a wide area. Linked together by passageways or patios protected from the sun's glare and the heat, the atmosphere is cool, almost airy. A retired former teacher runs the establishment on a voluntary basis. The teaching staff have agreed to a cut in wages to carry on offering classes without the financial backing of the French state.

The address of this 'other world'? Military Hospital 601 Square, Mezzeh. The last school building, at the north end, effectively adjoins the rear of Hospital 601. Fifty metres away, on the other side of the low perimeter wall, the hospital hangars have been emptied of cars and vans to make room for the mutilated and emaciated bodies that get piled up after being delivered from the detention centres. And it is there that the photographers from the military police compile their archives of death.

On 7 April 2015, Jérôme Toussaint, a respectable tour organizer, came to visit the staff and students at the school. A friend of the Syrian regime, this shadowy figure had already, six weeks earlier, arranged a trip to Damascus for four French parliamentary deputies on 25 February: Jacques Myard, a UMP member of the Foreign Affairs Committee at the Assemblée nationale, the PS deputy Gérard Bapt, Jean-Pierre Vial, a UMP senator and president of the Senate

France–Syria friendship group, and the UDI senator François Zochetto, a member of this group.[6] This visit, the first since the breaking off of diplomatic relations, was roundly condemned by François Hollande. Three of the French politicians met with Bashar al-Assad.

This time, Jérôme Toussaint was there as a member of the association SOS Chrétiens d'Orient [SOS Christians of the Orient], of which he was officially director of communications. He was leading a party of thirty or so pilgrims in the footsteps of their Syrian brothers in war. They attended Easter mass in Damascus, visited the fortress of Krak des Chevaliers in the centre of the country and the monastery of Maaloula. And they also dropped by the Lycée Français Charles-de-Gaulle, like the four French politicians before them. Reporters from the TV magazine programme *Complément d'enquête* on France 2 were following the trip.

So on this visit the group came to the Mezzeh quarter, arriving at the *lycée* from the south, without going via the roundabout in Hospital 601 Square, and mounted the broad stone steps that led up to the establishment. The guide stopped for a moment in front of the gate and explained to the journalists (the report was broadcast on 7 May 2015): 'When France decided to break off diplomatic relations, it left here like the USA quitting Saigon during the Vietnam War. But we have to think of the future; relations will not stay this way for another thirty years.'

---

6 UMP: Union pour un mouvement populaire (Union for a Popular Movement), party formed by a merger in 2002 by Jacques Chirac and renamed the Republican Party by Nicolas Sarkozy in 2015. PS: Parti socialiste (Socialist Party). UDI: Union des democrates et indépendents (Union of Democrats and Independents), centre-right party founded in 2012. [Trans.]

Was he unaware, this Frenchman who knew the regime and this city so well, that, on the other side of the street, people were being killed, no, assassinated in the name of this regime in a hospital whose very name sent a shiver down the spine of Syrians? Had he simply looked around him when he came to prepare this visit to the *lycée*?

In September 2013, as Western governments were pondering the possibility of a strike against the regime after the chemical attack on Damascus, the headmaster of the *lycée*, referring to the war and the bombardments not far from the centre of the capital, said on the radio station Europe 1: '[Here] people are able to bear the unbearable right on their doorstep.'

Tishreen, The Bunkered Hospital

Ahmad al-Riz
Was it his turn? Ahmad al-Riz's foot stank of death. His infected heel was giving off a smell of rotting flesh. Gangrene couldn't be too far away. Rumours about the hospitals circulated in the dark of the cells. You had to make sure you didn't go there. Most sick people who did never came back. Even those who weren't already dying.

Ahmad thought about his three friends who had died one after the other.

First, Ali, who was weakened by a very strong bout of diarrhoea. Before imprisonment he carried his 150 kilos lightly in the streets of the capital; now he barely weighed 70 kilos. On 23 December 2012, his pulse began to race. The *shawish* informed the jailer, who had him sent to the hospital at Tishreen. The next day he came back, still as weak as before. At the hospital they had done nothing but give him some glucose serum. He wasn't examined by a doctor, or even a nurse. His condition deteriorated. He was returned to the hospital and never came back.

Then there was Mustapha. He could barely breathe through his swollen mouth. His bread had to be dampened so that he was able to swallow it. He too was taken to hospital, and he too was returned very quickly. Unable to talk, unable to move. His friends carried him to the toilet so that he wouldn't do it all over himself, but his smell soon became unbearable. No one wanted to sit next to him. His wrecked stomach started to void itself. His breathing grew faster, then he passed away.

Finally, Marwan. Too weak to feed himself, he too was barely able to move. One day, in the toilets, he collapsed and died.

Like them, Ahmad al-Riz launched himself into the Revolution with all the energy of his twenty-five years. In spring 2011 he was studying IT in Damascus. Six months later, in the face of multiple arrests of pacifist militants, the activists tried to organize, developed secret networks and discovered how to encrypt information. Ahmad left for Lebanon to train with a foreign NGO. He learned how to secure his messages, organize a demonstration and protect himself and his family.

He was arrested on his way back, on 18 February 2012, and sent directly to Branch 215 of the military intelligence service. After seven days of interrogation under torture, then a week in solitary confinement on the fourth or fifth floor, he soon got to know the detention centre inside out. In the basement, eleven cells faced each other with no opening to the outside world. On one side the 'wood' cells, numbered 1 to 7; on the other side the 'iron' cells, numbered 1 to 4. Ahmad was in 'wood' cell number 3[7] with fifty to sixty other people. On the floor there was an army wool rug, brown, dirty,

---

7 See the sketch in Appendix 4.

infested with fleas and cockroaches. Outside it was still winter, but inside it was stifling.

After seven months of detention in different branches of the intelligence services and a parody of a trial, Ahmad landed up with about fifty other detainees in Saydnaya prison, about thirty kilometres north of Damascus, at 1,300 metres of altitude up in the mountains. In the courtyard, they got a pretty muscular reception: 'Get yourselves as naked as the day your whore of a mother pushed you out of her cunt!' Ahmad was locked up with ten or so men in the toilets, which measured one by one and a half metres. In the midst of the excrement, body pressed against body. Bottled up until the following morning. The worst was yet to come: promiscuity, lack of hygiene, rotten food ... After a year in this mountain prison, Ahmad al-Riz, eaten by fleas, no skin on his bones, with a piercing pain in his foot, oppressed by the heat of summer, saw death was approaching.

'Ahmad al-Riz! You're going to hospital!' They wrote four numbers in felt-tip on his forehead and, as was the case with Munir Abu Muaz, someone told him: 'You don't say your name there, just your number.' A number he no longer remembers today.

He was taken to Tishreen military hospital in a horsebox. Situated to the northwest of the capital, Tishreen is the second main hospital after Mezzeh. Ten or so buildings spread over twelve hectares. The main building is more than seven storeys high and extends for 200 metres. Bashar al-Assad, an ophthalmologist by training, practised there before he became president. Before the Revolution, the doctors there treated both military personnel and civilians. After an attack by the Free Syrian Army at the end of 2011, Tishreen was transformed into an entrenched camp. Tanks at ground level, snipers on the rooftops.

The room where Ahmad landed up was situated in a small building. On one side was a room reserved for sick people brought in from the detention centres. For those, like Ahmad, who came from Saydnaya, no beds, no toilets, and their food was simply thrown on the floor. In the room among the other sick people there was a thin man of about 30.

'Where do you come from?' Ahmad asked him.

'From Adra', he panted.

'What's the food like there?'

'We manage to get a bit to eat.'

'At Saydnaya we are hungry, very hungry.'

The man complained of stomach pains. His moans grew louder.

'Take him out into the corridor', ordered the jailer.

Ahmad did as he was told. He spread the man out on the floor outside the door. The next morning he found him lying in the same spot, a syringe in his forearm. Dead.

'Take this dog outside!'

With the help of another patient, Ahmad carried him to the hospital courtyard. With an ostensible look of disgust on his face, the jailer wrote a number with a marker pen on the body, took a photo and then asked them to put the corpse inside a transparent bag. Over the course of the afternoon, the jailer numbered and photographed five other bodies that Ahmad then placed in bags and carried to a van.

For a few months now, for security reasons on the roads, military police photographers such as Caesar had been unable to get to Tishreen. So the jailers, aided by the patients themselves, had had to adopt the routine: number on the body, photo, bag ... van ... destination unknown.

Ahmad was sent back to Saydnaya the next day. He had received no treatment. Three months later his condition had deteriorated, and he had to be brought back to Tishreen. Same building, same room. A man was lying on the floor, asking for water. An anonymous, inert form, barely breathing. The jailer asked for him to be placed in the corridor. By morning he too would be dead, a needle stuck in his arm. That day, Ahmad, the former student, placed a dozen bodies in bags and carried them to the van.

6

Caught in the Crossfire

Caesar

'I brought photos to Sami. I copied them onto a memory stick that he would provide me with, when I was alone in the office, constantly in fear that someone might come in and see me. When I left, I would hide the stick in my heel or my belt. To return home, I had to pass four or five roadblocks of the regime's army. I was very afraid. I didn't know what might happen to me. The soldiers might search me, even though I had an army identity card.

'During these two years, I was caught in the crossfire. I feared being arrested by the rebels because I worked for the regime and I feared being taken by the regime because I was collecting evidence about torture. I risked death on both sides, as did my family.

'Early in 2103 the situation in Damascus was getting tense. Our military complex was half encircled by the Free Syrian Army. It is a vast military complex, with military police, special forces, a part of the presidential guard, the military academy ... The rebels had taken the Berzeh quarter to the north and Tishreen to the east. They had posted snipers on the higher buildings in

69

Berzeh and they were firing down on us. The street that separated our complex from the Tishreen quarter was only four metres wide. This semi-encirclement lasted six months from the start of 2013.

'One morning I had to go to another office. While I was walking along, a sniper fired at me. I don't know if he was with the rebels or the army. The bullet missed me by a metre. In our office, as in all the others, after seven in the evening, when it got dark, we didn't turn on any lights so as not to provide a target.

'Before the war we entered the complex through the main door that opened onto the avenue bordering Berzeh. When the quarter was seized by the rebels, we had to find a different route. We came in via a passageway at the side, which was formerly secret and out of bounds because it crossed the military zone.

'Because of the conflict, lots of roads were cut off. For example, the staff who came from the centre of Damascus to work in Tishreen hospital could not come by their normal route any more. They had to make detours, drive along a mountain road on Mount Qassiun, where the regime had set up roadblocks. Their journey now lasted an hour, an hour and a half, instead of ten minutes. It had become quite risky to work at Tishreen. The hospital was often the target of mortar fire by rebels.

'It was the same for us. We could no longer go and photograph the bodies because of the security situation on the roads. What's more, with the increase in the number of bodies, a lot were sent to the hospital at Mezzeh, because it has a large garage and is in a zone that is totally under the control of the regime.

'For two years the most dangerous part for me was the journey to work and back. One morning, I left home around six o'clock. I was in a minibus, which we called the "services". The driver stopped, because there was firing on the road, and he didn't want to carry on. There were fourteen of us on the minibus, mostly workers. Our bosses, either civilian or military, told us we had to come to work, no matter what was happening on the roads. So we said to the driver: "We'll double your fare if you take us to the centre of Damascus."

'He hesitated, then, tempted by the price, he accepted. He took another route, which went through the mountains. But there we came across a Free Syrian Army roadblock. We weren't expecting that – their roadblock was just 700 metres as the crow flies from the regular army one. All the roads into Damascus had checkpoints. Car boots, women's handbags were opened, the buses were searched. In the end, before I fled the country, during summer 2013, they had women at the roadblocks to do body searches on women. The regime wanted to prevent people from the countryside and the surrounding towns getting into the centre of the capital.

'The first months of the Revolution, before the hate set in, I was told that the rebels and the army soldiers exchanged tea, mate or sugar. The rebels of the Free Syrian Army felt no hatred or aversion towards the agents of the regime. As they saw it, the regular soldier was bullied, forced to obey orders. But as the number of massacres of civilians by the regular army built up, the rebels stopped making excuses for them. The pursuit of the Revolution had become a matter of life or death on both sides.

'One morning, then, at the Free Syrian Army roadblock, there were four of them, with their multi-pocketed jackets and cagoules. One of them looked in through the window. I turned white as a sheet. I was very afraid that he would ask for our identity cards. I only had my army card. I didn't know the woman sitting next to me, but I started talking to her anyway, as if we were a couple. I thought that maybe that way he wouldn't try to speak to me.

'"Where do you come from?" the man asked the driver. "Do you have soldiers on board? *Mukhabarat*?"

'"I don't know."

'"All right, on your way."

'Another time, there was an opposition roadblock at the entrance to my town. I was on my way home. One of the rebels stopped the car and another verified my identity card. I recognized him. He was a mason who had done some work in my house. We got on well together. He knew I was working for the regime. At the roadblock he didn't say a word, he was actually quite nice and let me pass.

'It was all a bit strange, suspicious. "There must be some reason behind it." I got home feeling very stressed. I walked round and round in my living-room for half an hour, then I went back to see him. I had to know what was going on in his head. I took him to one side.

'"Why did you let me pass?"

'"Because I know you, but you should leave the regime."

'"It's difficult to desert. I've got my parents, my brothers and sisters. It would be suicide to leave the army before they were safe and sound."

'"Yes, I know. But be careful. Next time you might not find someone so understanding."

'So Sami decided to make me a civilian identity card to show at rebel roadblocks. My quarter was partly held by the Free Syrian Army.

'One Monday, we learned that the regime was going to lay siege to it. My family and I stayed put. Bashar's soldiers pillage the houses when they take over a town or a quarter. I didn't want to leave ours. My parents had saved up for years to buy it. The streets were deserted, sombre. Scary. There was no one left but a few old people and families who didn't know where to seek refuge. There was no more water, no more electricity. There was nothing but the sound of mortar fire.

'After three days, a close friend came to see me. He urged me to leave the quarter: "If the army see you they will believe you are a deserter because you are in a quarter defended by the opposition. And if the rebels find you they will take you because you work for the regime." We packed a few things in bags. My younger brothers carried them on their heads as if they might offer protection from the mortars. They were crying. We saw a truck with covers on the back. We climbed on board, then we set off. Just like in a film, with shells falling to the left and right.

'As we left the quarter, there was a checkpoint of the regular army to stop inhabitants from leaving. I got out of the truck and took the soldier to one side so that the driver wouldn't hear.

'"I'm a colleague."

'"So why are you inside?"

'"I came to find my parents."

'And I showed him my army card.

'When the siege was over we returned home. Our house had been destroyed and pillaged. The hardest thing was losing our souvenirs, our photographs. There were lots of things missing: the French crockery, with good-quality plates the colour of ivory, the Moulinex mixer and an automatic washing machine bought on credit. It had taken us two and a half years to pay off the loan of 25,000 Syrian pounds. My parents had bought everything on credit: the bedroom, the kitchen furniture … My mother loved cooking. She even had utensils she hadn't used yet.

'But Sami had saved the hard drive with all the copies of the photos.'

Hidden in the Trash

Sami regularly supplied Caesar with memory sticks. The first ones were four or eight gigabytes, but then later he used sixteen gigabyte sticks. Sometimes the military photographer was worried that he had 'missed' some photos. So he recopied all the month's pictures onto a CD, with the added risk of being found in possession of it.

Sami in turn transferred everything onto his two backups. First on the hard drive of his home computer, saving the documents in folders with anodyne names, in case an agent of the regime happened to come across them. Then onto an external hard drive. Long, crucial, essential minutes: only the original photos would provide metadata, with the date and the type of camera – proof of when the pictures were taken – and a high definition – so that the wounds could be analysed and a hypothetical cause of death established.

To make sure nothing was lost, the photos were sent abroad over the internet, in low definition this time, so the files weren't so big. Power cuts, bad connections, encryption of the data: the messages were sometimes hit and miss.

When the regime attacked their town, Sami got his wife and children out to put them somewhere safe. Then he came back to find one of his best friends, who had been in on the operation from the start. He was a wanted man for having put videos of demonstrations online and so hadn't been able to escape the encircled quarter. The two men took the computer and the hard drive, put them in a bag and hid them under a pile of trash – no question of risking a regular army checkpoint with that. They knew that the soldiers would not search where there was nothing to steal. 'In our hurry, we put all our eggs in one basket', Sami says with a smile.

When the mortar fire intensified and the first soldiers infiltrated the streets, the two friends went to hide in a neighbouring house. They hauled themselves up into a false ceiling in the kitchen and spent three anxious days and nights there. Sami thought about his family, his father, the rabbits he was raising on the roof of their house. They tried to see what was going on by peering through a gap in the wood. 'We saw soldiers forcing a young man to say: "There is no God but Bashar", then one of them shot him. We were afraid of dying like that. We weren't afraid of death, but dying in that way, yes.'

Staying Alive

Wafa and Sadiq

Death. Wafa escaped it and felt guilty about it. For having suffered less than the others too. Neither tortured nor raped. But she cries. Now in exile in Turkey, she is telling her story for the first time. Three days earlier, this former school employee was still in Syria and condemned to silence. Her husband had died in detention. His family still lived in a zone controlled by the regime, so were susceptible to arrest at any moment. For her testimony, she chooses to call herself Wafa, because the name means 'Faithful' in Arabic. For her husband, she uses the name Sadiq, which means 'Sincere'.

'He who enters is lost, he who leaves is reborn.' This could be a Syrian proverb, saying or prophecy. Like other witnesses, Wafa would repeat this phrase several times to express the state of mind of the Syrian people. 'When a person is arrested, you never know exactly when they will be set free. And when they come out – if they come out – it's like being born for a second time, for their family and for society, which have both changed do much since their arrest.'

In the Syria of Hafez al-Assad, more than 17,000 detainees disappeared between the late 1970s and the early 1980s. The human rights organization Syrian Network for Human Rights (SNHR) estimates the number of people detained since the start of the Revolution at 117,000, half of them without their families having any information about them. In its report of August 2015, the SNHR listed the figure of 215,000 detainees given by other local organizations.

Wafa and Sadiq were arrested at the same time, in May 2013. They had been anticipating it for a while. They had a suitcase ready packed for a quick getaway. At home, the couple, who had no children, watched foreign news channels such as Al Jazeera and Al Arabiya. Whenever they went out they switched channels on their set-top box in case an intelligence agent should come to check that they hadn't been accessing media which 'tarnished the image of their country'.

He was a civil servant who liked talking about freedom and pacifism. He had often warned young people against the temptation to carry arms, citing 'self-regard', 'recklessness' or 'influence'. 'He refused to express himself in the manner prescribed by the regime', his wife recalls. 'That is, accentuating the religious angle, saying that it is a sectarian revolution, led exclusively by Sunnis seeking to annihilate Alawites.'

On the morning of their arrest, the couple were waiting for a friend in the street with the intention of visiting a new apartment. They had a naive belief that moving house would be enough to keep them from danger. A patrol of Military Security turned up and made it clear they should get in the car, without bothering to check their identity cards. Clearly, they knew who they were. Wafa and Sadiq were taken to one of the branches of military intelligence. On the way, Sadiq was punched in the face several times. The agents seized their computers and mobiles and tried to take their money and the gold jewellery that Wafa was wearing.

In the office of the investigators, Wafa and Sadiq sat side by side. An officer came in and asked:

'Who's this?'

'So-and-so and So-and-so', a colleague replied.

'Why did you bring the wife? We don't want her. Give her back her identity card and let her go.'

'We might have need of her.'

'No, let her go.'

'Well, you're very kind-hearted, aren't you?'

The investigator went over and whispered a couple of words in his ear. The superior left. Wafa had to stay.

After a few questions, the couple had to stand outside in the corridor for several hours. They weren't allowed to speak to each other or look at each other. Then Sadiq was called back into the office. When he came out again he was blindfolded and dishevelled: his tie was gone and the tails of his shirt were outside his trousers. It was the last time Wafa saw her husband.

She was called in to see the investigator in turn. 'He asked me to undress. I was paralysed. Only my husband had seen me naked, and now I had to show myself to a stranger. I thought he was going to rape me. He only wanted to search me. I couldn't move, I couldn't even redo the buttons on my coat. It was as if my hands were anaesthetized.' The investigators assigned the number 24 to her and sent her to an overheated cell. Two women who were already in there tried to bunch up to allow her to lie down a little during the night. The next morning they took her up to the seventh floor, to a room measuring four square metres, with no windows, no beds, in which there were seven women. On the ground there were some thin, dirty blankets infested with cockroaches.

Detained at the Age of Three

As well as the women, there was Racha. Little Racha. She was three years old. She bore the number 8. On seeing her, Wafa, snapped and screamed: 'What has she done? You treat us as if we are already dead!' The child was with her mother. During the day, the women played with her – cooking or shopping, walking her round in little steps the two spare metres of the cell. 'Who's looking after my bird?' Racha asked over and over. 'Do you think she is dead now?' One afternoon the little girl put her face in the small window in the door, made a V for victory sign with her fingers and shouted in her childish language: '*Houliya!*' instead of '*Hourriya!*' 'Freedom.'

One of the jailers, a Druze, a minority in the country, was moved. Secretly, he slipped them a T-shirt from the prisoner in the cell opposite and brought Wafa some scissors and a needle.

On this spring morning in Istanbul, amidst tears of both joy and sorrow, Wafa takes out of her handbag a plastic bag containing a folded-up T-shirt with straps. She takes the little top out and, with infinite tenderness, smooths out the material with her hand. 'I sewed it for her so she would have something to change into when they washed her clothes. I also made her some shorts.'

Later, much later, after she was freed, when she looked at Caesar's photos that were published online, she recognized the jailer with the large moustache, who was called A.Z. 'He was the only guard who was nice to us. The others threatened us: "Watch out or you'll get yourself shot."' Wafa soon learned that her cell was a 'hotel' compared with those in the basement. Two meals a day, sometimes fresh fruit. 'We were privileged. We were allowed sanitary towels, whereas I was told elsewhere that girls used strips of rag, which they washed then reused still wet.'

78

Here on the seventh floor they had a tiny piece of soap between all of them. Wafa tried to maintain a minimal hygiene so that she wouldn't fall ill; she would wash her sole set of clothes – the ones she wore – and slip them back on while still damp. At night the eight women had to lie with their legs up the wall in order to lie flat on their backs.

The man in the cell opposite had been languishing in prison for more than twenty years. Another had been waiting for five years. 'They had been held there without trial', Wafa protests. 'They seem to have received an education. They weren't criminals. If they were the jailers wouldn't have dared go to sleep in the corridor. Right next to them.' Sometimes the doors of the cells were even left open.

Her interrogation sessions were not as Wafa had imagined sessions with the *mukhabarat* would be like. For many Syrians, torture was scarier than death. Wafa was not beaten, merely insulted. After a few weeks, her trips to the investigators' office became almost 'tokenistic'. They asked the same questions over and over without waiting for a reply: 'Do you belong to a humanitarian organization?' 'Your husband is a terrorist, he has organized car bomb attacks.'

The former school employee suspected that her husband was already dead and that they couldn't apply any more pressure on her to extract any confessions. The intelligence agents were simply seeking to keep her 'intact'. To extort some money from her family or to use her in a prisoner exchange. In the end, it would be both.

Human Shield

On the outside, the repression had taken a turn for the worse. On the morning of 21 August of that summer of 2013 a sarin attack killed more than 1,500 civilians in the plain of Ghouta. This farming suburb of Damascus had been under siege by the army for five months. Very soon there was no doubt as to the perpetrator. Only the regime possessed artillery rockets capable of delivering the chemical agent. The French intelligence services swung into action, the deputies of the European Parliament were up in arms.

Earlier, in the spring, 28 localized attacks had caused the death of at least seventy-three civilians. This time, faced with such a large number of victims in one place, the West could no longer turn a blind eye. France and the USA worked together. Barack Obama had threatened to intervene in Syria if the regime crossed the red line and used chemical weapons. An attack on the Syrian command structure seemed imminent. But Western capitals procrastinated. 'Punishment', 'vote', 'lack of evidence' … The USA backtracked and did not launch a strike.

In the detention centres of the Syrian capital they were preparing for sanctions. The officers had left the buildings. Next to her cell, Wafa could hear two jailers whispering to each other as they sat on the floor. 'If there are airstrikes, will we have to kill them?' The main door to the corridor was locked from the outside. The two men seemed worried. Normally not allowed mobiles on duty, they had theirs with them. But they were unarmed, apart from simple batons, and were panicking.

Everywhere there was a sense of haste. Mazen al-Hummada, the activist who became a *soukhra* in the military airport at Mezzeh, came out of his cell with several hundred other prisoners. Flanked by forty or so armed soldiers, they were led to the end of the runways. An officer who had deserted, a prisoner like him, walked alongside him. The knowledgeable officer was astonished to see the hangars empty of aeroplanes.

New doors had been installed at the entrances to the buildings. 'They put us in the hangars to act as a human shield', Mazen recounts today.

There was no airstrike. The old routine re-established itself.

A month later, Wafa went down to the investigators' office, where they promised her: 'You're going home.'

'What have you done with my husband?'

'He's been transferred to the justice system.'

'Why haven't I been before a judge? What are you going to do with me? I want my identity card, my computer, my house key.'

She wanted to get her possessions back. They demanded money. She refused and ended up exchanged. In the car that they ordered her to get into, two *shabiha*, militiamen of the regime, with shaven heads and tattoos, held grenades in their hands. Wafa would be traded for soldiers held prisoner by the insurgents.

When she got home, her family told her that one of her nephews – the one closest to her husband – had also disappeared. By bribing agents of the regime, he had found out very early on where the couple were being detained. For a few extra tens of thousands of Syrian pounds he had arranged for Wafa to speak to her brother on the phone. An extremely rare privilege. Another member of the family, who worked for the regime, had covered up for this phone encounter: 'Your family would like some reassurance.' Wafa, at the other end of the line, was very cautious: 'Everything is fine.'

For the nephew, the consequences were predictable: one morning, in the street, several *mukhabarat* stopped his car, made his wife get out and took him and his vehicle away. He was the third of three brothers to be arrested. The first had disappeared when he went out to buy some bread in the spring of 2013. The second had been imprisoned two and half months before the regime offered his parents the chance to pay money to see him in his hospital bed. Wounded in the head, he died only a few hours later.

So the person who had moved heaven and earth to find her and get her out was no longer around, and no one had heard anything about him since. Was he still alive? Was he one of those thousands of corpses photographed by the military police, like Sadiq? One of Wafa's friends had actually found the photo of her husband in Caesar's file and shown it to her: 'It was 24 June 2014', she recalls today, as if this day might stand in for the exact date when Sadiq died, which she would probably never know. She knows only one thing: 'When I saw the photo, I realized that he died very soon after our arrest. I had cut his hair the previous day. It hadn't had a chance to grow back very much. Nor had his beard.'

A year later, ten days before she left Syria for Turkey, Wafa prepared some dishes of pistachios and dried fruits to celebrate her brother's engagement. The families got together in her living-room, but their thoughts were elsewhere.

Her young brother opened his Facebook page on his computer, on which portraits of dead detainees had been posted. Photos from the Caesar file had begun to be disseminated through social media. Wafa's brother explained to them that this macabre and secret databank allowed those who had received no word of a brother, a husband, a daughter to receive confirmation of their death. The faces crowded round the screen. The photo of the third nephew was there, among the hundreds of others.

Today, from her refuge in Istanbul, Wafa continues to scrutinize the thousands of photos from Caesar that are in circulation on internet sites. Unable to 'return to [her] previous life', 'ashamed of having got off so lightly', 'determined not to forget the suffering of others'. It is her way of participating. 'We are responsible for what happens today', the survivor suggests. To be silent and let the dictators speak for us is to give them a blank cheque. Our silence after the events in Hama has brought us to where we are. How many families still don't know to this day what happened to their loved ones during this massacre?'

7

With the Families of the Disappeared

Caesar

'I sometimes helped mothers search for their sons. They came to ask me when they had tried everything else. They had followed up contacts that led nowhere or paid out money for nothing in return.

'In our country, people have always had to pay to get information on their loved ones in detention. After the Revolution, this corruption took on a whole new dimension. Inside the army and the intelligence services, authority was fractured, orders were not always respected, the pillars of the regime had to some extent disintegrated. This mafia became a sort of jungle. Many saw a chance to make even more money from selling information, including false information. Even the most minor question to a member of the regime came with a price tag attached, as did every minor reply.

'Before the war, if you had paid money and got ripped off, you could lodge a complaint. Today that is impossible. When a father tries to find out where his arrested son, whom he hasn't heard from in months, is, he will try to see an officer, an intelligence agent or a lawyer connected to the regime. And if this person extracts money from him on the promise of having his son released but doesn't keep his word or lies to him because his son is already dead, what can the father do about it? Complain to the authorities? He'll just be told: "You're seeking information about a terrorist? You're a terrorist too. You brought up your son to be a terrorist. You should be put in prison too!" The agents all cover each other's back.

'So the mothers tried to get information through a go-between. As I was not especially high-ranking, I had less power than the others. They came to me when they were desperate. When they called me on my mobile, it was risky, because my phone was tapped. So I called them back from one of the public telephones that wasn't monitored. I could get information from a few friends. When detainees leave the detention centres they pass through the hands of the military police before they go to prison. But I knew nothing about what happened in the detention centres.

'Helping these families made me feel better. My conscience was clear even though I still worked for the regime, for Bashar al-Assad.

'When someone is looking for information about a loved one arrested by military intelligence, for example, in theory they go to military justice. If the prisoner is dead, they are directed to Tishreen hospital, where the medical examiners' records are kept, to get a death certificate. If he is in prison, they are sent to the military police to get a visitor's permit. If he is held by one of the branches of the intelligence services, then a veil is drawn over the whole thing and they are told that there is no information available.

'That's when having good contacts and a bit of money come into play.

'In the two years when I was photographing the bodies of detainees, about ten or so families came to us directly. If you have the number of the detainee himself, or his medical record number, it is possible to track down the photo in our archives. But without one of these numbers it's impossible, as we don't file these photos by the name of the deceased.

'One day a man came looking for the photo of his brother. He was accompanied by an investigator of the military police and by the head of our department. He had obtained his brother's detention number. He recognized his brother from a tattoo and a gold tooth. He was the father of two children. As he left, in shock, he offered the investigator some money. The latter refused to accept it in front of me, but I'm sure he got hold of it later.

'Another day, two women came to our office, again with an investigator and an IT person. They were sisters-in-law. The man they were looking for was the husband of one and the brother of the other. They were about thirty, thirty-five years old. They had a form signed by the intelligence services with the number of a medical examiner. Thanks to this number, I was able to know what day the man was photographed. It was easy to find because the photos are listed by this number and by date. There were thirty or forty photos on file for this particular date.

'When they saw the photo they started to scream, to tear at their faces, to pull out their hair. It was really hard, because I couldn't say anything or show that I understood their pain. And they weren't able to insult the regime that had killed their husband and brother. They would have been arrested too. One of them fainted. An agent went to get some eau de Cologne to revive her. I remember it well, it was the first year of the Revolution, because then soldiers could still get hold of eau de Cologne. Later, it became too expensive because of the war.

'Another time, some members of the regime contacted the family of a boy in detention. They promised to release him in exchange for half a million Syrian pounds (about 3,300 euros at the time). The boy's father knew someone in the military police. This police officer told him that his son was definitely dead and that they shouldn't pay a penny. The father didn't want to believe him and was ready to pay the money.

'The police officer came to see me and we had a look. We had an approximate date of death. We searched through the photos and we found him. When we saw the body, we realized that he had died shortly after his arrest. The policeman used his mobile to photograph one of the photos from the boy's file, the one of the lower half of his body, which was recognizable because he was wearing underpants with a distinctive chess-board design on them. I didn't want him to copy the other photos, especially the one of the face. I was very afraid that his parents would go to complain to the security services who were trying to extract money from them when the young man was already dead. The police officer swore to me that he would erase this photo from his phone so that there was no risk of either of us being arrested.

'In Syria, when someone is arrested, they are tortured and might reveal information, whether true or false, which sends ten other people to prison. Even if they have no connection to the case.'

Money for any Piece of Information

Ahmed
When Khaled died, his body was marked on the forehead with a number and a name: '9077' and '*Jawiyye*' ('Air', signifying 'Air Force Intelligence Services'). The medical examiner assigned the number 3217 to him

for his medical report. On the photo, Khaled shows no obvious sign of torture, his face is recognizable, despite a burn around one eye and a week and a half's worth of stubble. The only giveaway: one of his feet is red. Khaled is still wearing the pyjama tops and bottoms he had on under his clothes when he went to the butcher's. It was cold on that morning of 2 January 2013 when a patrol of Air Force intelligence stopped him in the street. It was his second arrest.

This 42-year-old father was a works foreman from Daraya, a middle-sized town on the outskirts of Damascus. About ten kilometres southwest of the centre of the capital and near to the military airport at Mezzeh, this town of 250,000 inhabitants was at the forefront of the pacifist movement. From the early days of spring 2011, the young people of Daraya marched in silence to demand the release of prisoners of conscience. Some of them chanted: *'Silmiye, silmiye!'* ('Peaceful, peaceful!'). Others offered flowers or water to the regime's soldiers.

Khaled's first arrest took place in his office in March 2012. A little while later, a detainee liberated by intelligence services posted a list of his former cellmates on a Facebook page dedicated to Daraya, to inform family, friends and loved ones in the most efficient manner possible. It is not enough to simply understand the prisoners' descent into hell in the darkness of the cells without entering into the silence into which their disappearance casts their mothers, their brothers or their children. The cruelty of absence, the violent arrogance of the intelligence services. Passing on news about detainees is risky work, but essential.

In the 1980s, thousands of Islamists were locked up in Palmyra prison, in the middle of the desert, without their families being informed. A number of them died of hunger or under torture. Or were summarily executed in their cells, as on 27 June 1980, the day after a failed assassination attempt against Hafez al-Assad, when the army entered the prison and killed 1,000 detainees.

And even today, anyone who enters the door of a detention centre disappears. Sometimes, to protect an exhausted mother or an old father, their family conceal the arrest of their son or daughter. And if their death is confirmed, it is hushed up too. A secret death. Memory forbidden.

So when the Daraya detainee got out, he posted the name Khaled on social media. Ahmed, the brother, asked him: 'Are you sure it's really him?' Yes, it really was Khaled. Another friend put him in contact with an agent of the regime, who, for 400,000 Syrian pounds (about 4,000 euros at the time), secretly recorded Khaled's voice in order to play it to his family. 'I recognized it immediately', Ahmed confirmed. Five months later, Khaled would be freed. To return to a painful and violent reality.

A few weeks later, pacifist Daraya experienced one of the worst massacres of the war. More than 700 inhabitants were executed in punitive reprisals against the town on 25 and 26 August 2012. The local imam, who preached non-violence, had already been arrested. Ghyath Mattar, a twenty-six-year-old man who handed roses to soldiers, had been tortured to death and his body returned to his family. A death that had moved the American State Department. But Daraya was unbowed and persisted in its demand for democracy. On 20 August, the army massed troops around the town, blocked entry and exit points and began to bombard the neighbourhoods. Lines of communication were cut off. The *shabiha*, the regime's militia, infiltrated the town, combed the streets, massacred worshippers in mosques, executed anyone who dared set a foot outside, slaughtered whole families on stairwells.

The next day, the streets were strewn with victims. Men, women, children, old people. On the state TV channel Addounia, the presenter spoke about a massacre perpetrated by 'terrorists' and confirmed that the army had cleaned the streets of 'armed gangs', then introduced the report of the journalist on the spot. Sunglasses perched on top of her head, her blue top matching her bulletproof vest, her shoulder bare, the beautiful journalist addressed the viewers: 'As you can see, dear viewers, there are victims everywhere. I don't know if I can find words sufficient to describe this ... Look, here is a woman who is still alive. Let's talk to her and hear what she has to say ...'

A grotesque piece of reportage. Obscene. The journalist stepped over corpses, pointed her microphone at an old woman lying injured in the cemetery. She had lost her husband, her daughter and her two sons. The reporter continued on her way to interview a little three-year-old girl sitting in a pick-up truck, frozen in shock next to her mother's dead body. With a backing track fit for an action movie, with both slow-motion and fast-motion sequences, she followed the soldiers who opened fire on their mission to 'disinfect the area of remaining terrorists'.

Surrounded by soldiers, the witnesses parroted the official line.

During the attack, a paternal uncle of Khaled, a respected imam who preached non-violence, was arrested. The rest of the family fled the town and based themselves a few kilometres to the north, in the Mezzeh quarter of Damascus. Three of the six brothers, their wives and their children all shared a large, seven-roomed house. That 2 January 2013, when Khaled did not return with the shopping, his brother Ahmed realized what had happened. The tobacconist confirmed that an informer had denounced him to the *mukhabarat*. A patrol from Air Force Intelligence had come to arrest him.

Ahmed again got in touch with an intermediary. A retired officer this time. In the café where they met he slipped him an envelope containing 1,500 dollars. 'Give me a bit of time, I'll see what I can do', the man promised him. Ahmed caught up with him a week later, in the same place. 'Your brother is OK. The jailers have been told not to beat him. If you want to get him out, the head of the branch is asking for 1,500 dollars.' Ahmed got together some more of his savings and sold a gold bracelet belonging to his wife. A few weeks later he met the retired officer again. 'They've done a report so that he won't be convicted as a terrorist.' Six weeks passed. 'Be patient', the former military man advised him. The next time, he assured him: 'He's doing fine. No one is harming him. He'll be released at the next amnesty.'

In fact, Khaled had been dead for a while. He was killed less than two weeks after his arrest, according to the photo taken by Caesar or one of his colleagues. But his family had not given up hope. 'What choice did we have?' Ahmed explains today, having sought refuge in Turkey with the rest of his family.

A year earlier, money had ensured the release of Munser, the youngest of the brothers. He had been sentenced to fifteen years for terrorism and locked up in Saydnaya prison, but the money had been used to bribe a corrupt judge, who freed him. One of his uncles had also benefitted from such an arrangement. After three months in detention, the old man had been transferred to the civilian prison at Adra, then released. Today he is no longer of sound mind, partially blind and can only hear in one ear. His stay in Hospital 601 at Mezzeh, where he was chained to his bed, with a shoulder dislocated and suffering hallucinations, had left its mark. 'It's a simpler procedure when our loved ones are in prison', Ahmed explains. 'The lawyer can make sure the money gets to the right person. It's more opaque and risky when they are in a detention centre. We never know where our agent is going or which go-betweens are of any use.'

Common Graves

The imam uncle who was arrested during the massacre of Daraya was not set free. He died five months after his arrest. His photo was found among the collection posted on the internet by Caesar. He bore the number 3026 and the inscription '*Jawiyye*'. On 1 November 2012, the medical examiner filed him under the number 2409. Like him, Khaled's body was dumped in the hangar of Hospital 601 at Mezzeh. His decease was recorded in the medical report under the number 3217 in January 2013. At this time, all his family had found refuge in this residential quarter after the Daraya massacre. They were living less than 500 metres from the hospital.

Khaled's body was there, just a few minutes on foot from their house of refuge, awaiting burial in a mass grave. But, as with all the other thousands of civilians murdered in the detention centres, Khaled's 'funeral' was organized and recorded. For example, here is the interment order for one Y.M.[1]

Top secret
Syrian Arab Republic
General Command of the Army and Armed Forces
Intelligence Division – Branch 227
Number: XXXX/5T
Date: XX/XX/2013

---

[1] The original document can be seen in Appendix 3.

To the Military Police, Damascus

At the time of the inquiry, the individual arrested, Y.M., first name of the mother B., resident in the quarter of S., opposite the town hall.

His health having deteriorated, he was admitted as an emergency to Hospital 601 on XX/XX/2013.

The above-mentioned person died following cardiac arrest and respiratory failure. His body was stored in the cold store of the above-mentioned hospital under the number X/XXXX.

Please inter his body in a suitable place in coordination with the office in charge of burying the dead, in conformity with the decision of the Office of National Security in the Branch 248 file, number XXXXX/XXX/X, dated XX/XX/2012, which was sent to you and in your knowledge.

Attached: a stamped envelope with a red seal containing the identity card of the accused.

Copies to:
Branch 291/B with reference to letter number XXXXX
Branch 248 with reference to the letter from Branch 291/B mentioned above
Branch 294 with reference to the letter from Branch 291/B mentioned above

Number of copies: 5

Divisional head of the intelligence service
By power of attorney
Head of Branch 227

Where was Khaled buried? In the 'martyrs' cemetery' in Najha? In the 'southern cemetery' in Bahdaliyah? These two cemeteries on the southern outskirts of Damascus are suspected of containing common graves.

In collaboration with Human Rights Watch, the Syrian human rights organization Violations Documentation Center, in a report of September 2013 on Branch 215 of military intelligence, published incriminating eyewitness statements and satellite photos: the arrival of refrigerated trucks, landfill works using bulldozers, traces of piles of sand and lime, which can dissolve bodies ...

According to witness reports collected by Violations Documentation Center,[2] one day in late September or early October 2012, two trucks entered Najha cemetery. Hundreds of bodies would have been buried there. The security forces had barred access to the site by closing off streets with roadblocks, but there were already eyewitnesses present nearby.

---

2 http://www.vdc-sy.info/index.php/en/reports/ 1380463510#.VZT3ePntmko.

8
A Duty to Get Out Alive

Caesar

'We wanted to release these photos so that the families of the dead men could know whether their loved ones had died. People needed to know what was happening in the prisons and the detention centres. When Bashar al-Assad falls, the regime will want to destroy all evidence, that is for certain.

'Why does the regime keep all these photos? I've often asked myself that. Why describe the bodies and keep their photos? I'm just a simple man, not a politician, so can only give a simple answer. The regime's intelligence and security services are not particularly coordinated. Each is ignorant of what the other is doing. They each organize themselves and operate according to their own principles. Military justice, the security services …

'For fifty years, the military police has been archiving evidence of accidents and deaths of soldiers for military justice. In other words, documenting deaths. The photos are used by judges and investigators. They make the file more definitive. If the judges have to reopen it one day, they will need them. At the start of the Revolution and during the war, we were quite simply continuing the same routine. The regime never imagined its system could be used against it.

'The security services have a feeling of total impunity. They don't imagine that they will ever be held to account for their atrocities. They know that the major powers are propping up the regime. They also never imagined that the photos would leak out and be shown to the outside world.

'In fact, I sometimes wonder if the heads of the security services are stupider than we think. They were so busy suppressing demonstrators, pillaging the people, killing, that they forgot that their atrocities were being documented. Look at the chemical attack on Ghouta! Those responsible knew that there would be documentary evidence. And yet they still made the attack!

'But what is the fundamental reason for photographing all these bodies that have been tortured to death? Only the regime can properly answer that question. I'm sure that they are still doing it, in spite of all the photos I have smuggled out.

'Just as I am sure that the members of the regime continue to believe that the demonstrators and the rebels of the Free Syrian Army are "terrorists", egged on by exterior forces, and that they are destroying the country. At the start of the Revolution, the majority of the military thought that way. Many later realized that it wasn't true, but so much blood had already been spilled.

'I can remember when the regime freed the jihadists who had fought against the Americans in Iraq. They had been arrested when they returned to Syria. In our department we were all surprised. Why had the regime done that?

'I didn't speak with them personally, but they were processed though the headquarters of the military

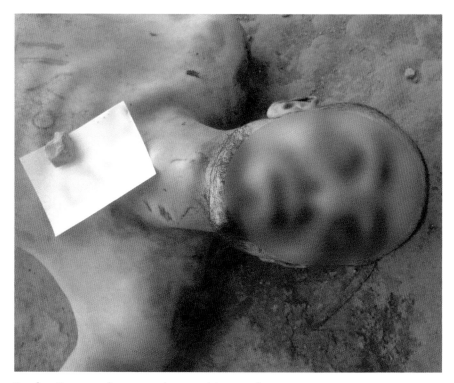

In the Caesar photographs, a white card or paper
on each body indicated the security branch number,
detainee number (assigned by the security branch), and
medical examination number (assigned by a medical
examiner after death).

(Previous page) Groups of bodies waiting
to be photographed and logged by military
medical personnel, in the garage of Military
Hospital 601 in Mezzeh, Damascus.

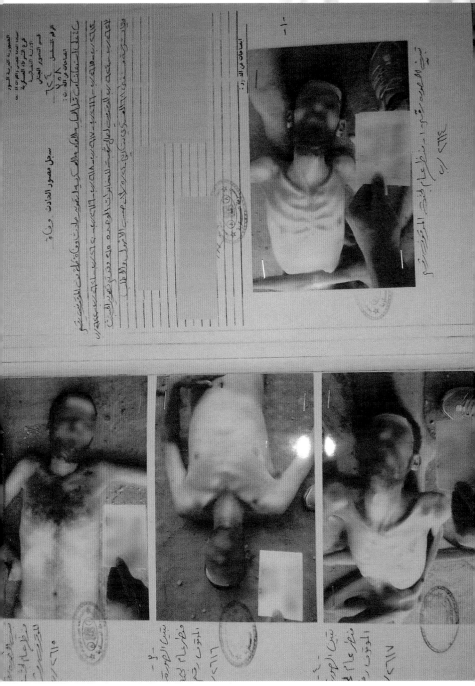

A medical report smuggled out by Caesar outlines the procedure after detainees' bodies were removed from security branches. The report states: 'based on the order of the military general prosecutor, photographs of the bodies of … prisoners under responsibility of the security services, unit 215, in the Morgue of the Military Hospital 601 on 24 May, 2013, based on these orders.'

Members of the Syrian Organisation for the Victims of War (SOVW) display photos by Caesar at an exhibition in Geneva on 17 March 2016.

Exhibition of the Caesar photographs at the UN headquarters in New York, March 2015.

Caesar, in a blue hooded jacket, waits to brief the House Committee on Foreign Affairs in Washington DC, 31 July 2014.

police. Prisoners who are about to be freed, thanks to an amnesty, for example, are transferred to us. The military intelligence services and the Ministry of the Interior send an order to the military police and the civilian police.

'The detainees come to us in trucks with bars. They are assembled in the courtyard and are kept in the prison of the military police for between twenty-four and forty-eight hours before being taken in front of a judge, who sets them free.

'The policemen in charge of supervising them were speaking amongst themselves. They were wondering how the regime could free men who had fought in Iraq. They didn't understand.

'During the two years I was making clandestine copies of these documents, I was afraid for my family and for myself. I had started something and I couldn't go back. I had to see it through to the end. I knew that one day I would stop this work, but I didn't know when. I put off the moment. But it became inevitable, I had to leave.

'One day, I felt that I was in greater danger than ever before. The decision was made to get me out. It was hard. I was anxious beforehand. But we had already lost our house and our belongings and had been living in accommodation lent to us by an acquaintance.

'I never thought I would be forced to leave my country. Before the Revolution, we led a simple, modest life; we had no great ambitions. We had never visited the beautiful parts of Syria. We never had the time or the money. I had only been to the cinema twice in my life. I had never travelled abroad. I didn't have a passport. Conscripts on National Service, soldiers and members of the intelligence services are not authorized to travel.

'My parents' generation all lived through the regime of Hafez al-Assad, and then that of his son. You aren't allowed to do anything without the authorization of the security services. In every aspect of daily life – marriage, divorce, travel, even naming children – you need permission. The Syrians have got used to living with this injustice. It has become a staple of their lives. They have borne the burden. When pain accumulates, the human being learns to live with it.

'One morning, I was in the office. I was sleeping there because by then we were a bit understaffed. We weren't allowed to go home. I had a job to do that would allow me to pass the roadblocks in Damascus and on its outskirts. My escape had been planned for that moment. I was going to leave and not come back.

'When I set foot outside the military police building I felt both sad and happy. Sad to be leaving behind friends I had worked with for so long. Sad to be heading off into the unknown. But happy to be escaping the daily stress involved in photographing the bodies and running the risk of being arrested. We never knew what tomorrow had in store for us.

'As I went through the gate of the military complex, I didn't think about my parents, I was just thinking about getting myself to safety: how could I reach the border in one piece? I was too afraid. I was slightly reassured that I had a legitimate mission that allowed me to move relatively freely and pass the roadblocks in Damascus and the suburbs.

'I had a rendezvous with a member of the opposition at a bus station. Someone had described him to me, and he too knew what I looked like. We had each other's phone number just in case, even though mine was tapped. It was risky. I was afraid that he would betray me, and he was afraid that I might be a spy still in the pay of the regime. Fortunately, I knew the area, and that reassured me. We recognized each other. With barely a word, we got into his car and drove off.

'I was surprised that he knew so many people. We

went through a few roadblocks without being asked for our papers. Then we headed off to a minor road, a rather stony, unfrequented route, in order to get out of Damascus. After about fifty kilometres, he handed me over to another person, who handed me over in turn to someone else whom I didn't know. I got a new handler about every fifty kilometres. It's the only way you get around in Syria today. You need men who know the area, the roads and the unguarded routes, so you can avoid the roadblocks. But these handovers where I changed car and handler were always nerve-racking. "Will this one betray me? What about him? Am I in safe hands?"

'On the road, in territory controlled by the rebels, it seemed safer, but there were regime informers everywhere. The journey lasted several days. We crossed war zones.

'And I arrived at the southern border. I stayed there for a while in the home of a trusted person with his wife and children. She knew I was a deserter but didn't know what I had done. This region was known for helping deserters and was encircled by the regime.

'I had to wait for the opportune moment to try to illegally cross the border. After a few days, I began to get bored stuck in the house. I went out and saw agencies distributing food aid to civilians. Flour, milk. It came from Arab countries and Western countries. One day, at the exact time that the food was being distributed, a mortar shell fell twenty metres away from us. It couldn't have been a coincidence. So the army must have had its informers here!

'Gradually the family accepted me as one of their own. I felt like I was a burden – there were quite a few of them, and there was not enough food to go round. The grandmother made the bread herself, because the bakery had been destroyed by the regime.

'There, I discovered what it was like to live with hunger in an area under siege. In Damascus, in the areas controlled by the regime, there was bread, and the means to buy food. We didn't realize that some people in Syria were suffering from hunger. Here, people had to queue for hours to receive a small bag of food. I never imagined I would experience that.

'I went out sometimes during the day, to gardens in the neighbourhood. I collected grapes. The local people are generous. I didn't have to go far. One evening the man of the family came home and didn't see me there. He got angry when I came back. He had been afraid that I had fallen into the wrong hands – regime informers or armed extremist groups.

'I crossed the border hidden in a car. When I got to the neighbouring country I found several members of my family. I was happy to see them and to know that they were safe. But the place was swarming with informers, you couldn't rest easy. Several deserters had been killed there. We were careful not to mix with the large number of other Syrians who had sought refuge there.

'We stayed several months before seeking refuge in Europe. I was afraid of the future, I was anxious. When we left, Sami's children were happy to be on the plane. When it landed and the door opened onto the footbridge, they dashed out, full of joy. Children have no idea of what awaits them.'

Urgent Exfiltration of Caesar

Sami, Abu Khaled
Caesar can't describe how he was protected. In the early summer of 2013, rebels from the Free Syrian Army kept a discreet watch on him. Without his knowledge, fighters had been following his slightest movements

from a distance for months. Their commander was Abu Khaled, a small, slightly built man of few words. He was from Qalamoun, like Abu al-Leith, the survivor of Branch 227 of military intelligence.

On two occasions, Abu Khaled and his group had 'lost' informers. They had been unmasked by the regime before being able to smuggle out evidence of crimes which they had collected in the military hospitals of Mezzeh and Tishreen.

It was now two years since the Revolution had broken out and the country had been plunged into civil war. The map of Syria looked like a leopard skin: patches controlled by the regime, patches of territory held by the opposition, who were attempting to set up a new administration, such as in the north, near the Turkish border. Some front lines had become stable. Others shifted constantly. It was no longer possible to travel from one town to another by the normal road. Not only did you have to be aware of where the enemy's roadblocks were, but you also had to know the tracks and paths that allowed you to avoid them, even if it meant a detour of several hours ... or days.

The jihadists of Daesh, Islamic State, joined the fray in Syria in spring 2013. Gradually they nibbled away at the territory held by the rebels of the Free Syrian Army in the northeast of the country; they seemed more interested in fighting the opposition than the regime. The regime too was more inclined to attack the military positions of the FSA, which held out the prospect of a moderate political alternative to the power of Bashar al-Assad, than those of Daesh. Daesh and the regime made common cause against a democratic future.

It was becoming a matter of urgency to get Caesar out of the country. Caught in the crossfire, he was perpetually living on the edge, tortured by guilt at being somehow complicit in the regime's massacres. Several times he had wanted to stop, several times he was persuaded to go on. Only he could collect the evidence on the inside of the regime itself. His friend Sami was in contact with an activist of the moderate and peaceful opposition who collected the stolen photos and sent them abroad in encrypted messages. Thousands had already been collected and sent in this way. Was it worth continuing, with the constant risk that Caesar might be discovered, when he was the key witness of Bashar al-Assad's death machine?

In the day-to-day unfolding of the war and the continuation of the operation, the sensitivity of the file was not immediately apparent. To fully appreciate the photos, you had to take the time to see them up close, to scroll through them slowly. To realize that those young men with big smiles on their faces and surgeon's gloves on their hands are soldiers of the regime, Syrians, and they are squatting down, posing in front of the dead bodies of other Syrians. And then to stop, appalled, as you see the photo of a neighbour or a cousin.

Sami had known that pain. He knew how effective it is. He decided to send Abu Khaled the photo he had located on the hard drive of one of his doctor friends, imprisoned by the regime. In wartime Syria, all health professionals are persecuted. Because they care for the wounded no matter who they may be – peaceful demonstrators, armed rebels, inhabitants of quarters held by the opposition, sometimes even militia men fighting for the regime – they are considered by those in power as 'terrorists'. The UOSSM (the Union of Syrian Medical Relief Organizations) has a list of 292 doctors killed since May 2011.

From the early months of the Revolution the public hospitals were no longer places of safety. Activists would have their hands amputated for no reason, lightly injured demonstrators would be left to die. To properly treat civilians, surgeons had to resort to operating in secret, in kitchens, in cellars, cramped spaces with inadequate hygiene and completely lacking in anaesthetics, disinfectants, dressings, scalpels, lancets …

Like the activists and armed rebels, many healthcare providers adopted false names to avoid being tracked down and to protect their families. In the areas controlled by the opposition, the hospitals were deliberately targeted by the regime's rockets and missiles.

It is as dangerous to be a doctor, nurse or medical assistant in today's Syria as it is to carry a Kalashnikov on the front line.

So Sami was very aware of what he was doing when he emailed the photo of this doctor's dead body to Abu Khaled. The man had been pulled up at a loyalist army roadblock while on the way to see the commander of the FSA. Tortured to death, his face swollen, his body broken, the photo of his corpse found its way via the official route into the archives of the military police. Then, via Caesar, onto Sami's hard drive. And finally onto the computer of Abu Khaled. The shock.

The next morning, Sami took the road that led to Abu Khaled's family farm in the heights of Qalamoun, on an isolated mountain top overlooking several other hills, providing natural defences against invaders. There, the two men had a long conversation. 'We absolutely had to help Caesar desert', Abu Khaled relates today. 'We had to get him out of the country in one piece, and these photos had to be seen by the whole world.'

Abu Khaled organized the exfiltration of the anonymous hero. Caesar crossed the border hidden inside a car. There were tens of thousands of files saved on two hard drives. One of them, which contained copies of photos already sent by email in low definition, was already abroad. The other, with the original photos in high definition, was still in Syria. Abu Khaled would secretly cross the mountains on the Lebanese border to smuggle it out. Before handing it over to Sami in Beirut.

The moment of revelation was close at hand, the moment of justice would soon follow.

Transmitting the File

Hassan Shalabi
Several weeks after their escape, in a country neighbouring Syria, Caesar, Sami and his family lived like refugees in a borrowed apartment.

Hassan Shalabi, a long-time opponent of Bashar al-Assad, entered the dimly lit room, icy cold on this early winter day – the electric heating worked only sluggishly – and in the gloom gave Caesar a big hug. For this Syrian, the general secretary of the Syrian National Movement, which worked towards the peaceful overthrow of the Syrian regime, what the deserter had achieved was a miracle. A moderate Islamist grouping, the Syrian National Movement, created in 2011 by university lecturers and scientists, championed values of freedom, democracy, social justice and equality, through a prism of Islamic principles.

In this winter of 2013 governments and public opinion in the West spoke of nothing but 'jihadists', 'terrorists' and 'Islamic State'. In the north of Syria, in the so-called 'liberated' territories, a dozen foreign journalists had been kidnapped by the future butchers of Islamic State.

'The world conflated the real revolutionaries and the jihadists', Hassan Shalabi explains. 'They forgot about the terrorism on the part of the state that started all this off and continues to this day.' Now, with Caesar's photos, he has a means of illustrating this state terrorism. The evidence speaks for itself and will – he believes – shift the conflict away from the military sphere – where no side is able to gain the upper hand – and into the law courts and international tribunals.

Hassan Shalabi learned about the file via a friend of Sami whom he had known from childhood. Indeed, from childhood, this forty-two-year-old researcher in Islamic sciences with a degree in management has not been able to tolerate the thought of families not knowing the whereabouts of a relative who has been arrested. This had been his own family's experience.

It was a Friday in December 1980. The children were squabbling in the family car. There were seven of them, the eldest girl was eight years old, the baby two months. Hassan, the eldest boy, was seven.

They had driven from the town of Al-Tal, where they lived, about ten kilometres from Damascus, to visit their maternal uncle at Berzeh, to the west of the capital. The blue Honda parked outside the uncle's apartment building. The little gang jostled each other to get out of the car. Their mother, the baby in her arms, urged them to get a move on. Their father, who had already stepped out, stood waiting in front of the vehicle.

'*Salam aleikoum*. Can we ask you something, brother?' Two men in civilian clothes, dark-grey trousers, brown pullovers, spoke to the father, Abu Hassan ('the father of Hassan' in Arabic, an affectionate diminutive that Arabs often give to parents). The man approached them. With a sudden movement they pulled a hood over his head, hit him with a baton and threw him into a Jeep, which had parked a little further along the road and now pulled up.

'Abu Hassan *rah!*' the mother cried in tears. Her husband had 'gone', in the expression used in the 1980s, when so many disappeared into the maw of the intelligence services. The passers-by in the street all froze. No one dared to come over to them to offer comfort.

'Hassan', the mother shrieked, 'go and find your uncle!' The uncle was adamant: 'Don't ever mention this to anyone. No one must know he has been arrested.' Then he ushered everyone inside the house. And he was an army officer. If he ordered them to be silent, who on earth would come to their aid?

During the distressing weeks that followed, the family begged the uncle to find out what had happened. He claimed that he had tried, but to no avail. Young Hassan, who listened to all these discussions from the lofty vantage point of his seven years, was fearful. If this officer was afraid of the security services, then his father was lost.

Thirty-four years later, history would catch up with the officer, now a grandfather. His own son would be arrested and tortured to death to punish the family for the activism of Hassan, who had fled the country and was acting as advocate for Caesar's file. His wife went to reclaim the body for burial. The reply was unequivocal: 'We have buried him ourselves.' So no body, just a form to sign declaring that her husband died of a 'cardiac arrest' during an interrogation. The form would serve as a death certificate, so that the wife could settle her husband's estate. That was it. No goodbye, no grave to visit.

In the street that Friday in December 1980, the young Hassan hadn't said goodbye to his father either. After childish tears, a yawning void to which later would be added a silent anger at his mother's resignation. And that he would put to use in helping the families of the disappeared.

'I didn't understand', Hassan Shalabi recalls today. 'My father was a very popular professor of Islamic sciences. He was a religious man, a devout man who helped others a lot. He didn't like the Muslim Brothers, because he didn't agree with politicizing Islam, but, like them, he was an opponent of the regime.'

Abu Hassan was sent to the prison in Palmyra. Like thousands of prisoners of conscience. For three months, until he was freed, his family would receive no news about him. The day after his return, the father sent everyone to Saudi Arabia. 'He had realized that he had only been released so that they could better keep tabs on him, especially when he established contact with his opposition friends again', his son explains. 'My father left the country clandestinely and came and joined us. I grew up in Saudi Arabia and didn't set foot in Syria again until the age of twenty-four.'

Hassan married a Syrian woman who came from Al-Tal, like him, and moved to Damascus. He was driven by his obsession to help the families of prisoners find out where their loved ones were being incarcerated and how they were being treated. To give them a hand, not leave them in ignorance as he had been at the age of seven, abandoned with his family, invisible before the authorities' wall of silence.

In the late 1990s, Hassan met Imad Eddine al-Rachid, one of his wife's professors (she was continuing her studies). He taught Islamic sciences at the faculty of Sharia in Damascus, of which he would become vice-dean. The two men liked each other.

Like Hassan, Imad grew up in a family imbued with social justice and Muslim values. Like him, his formative years were his adolescence. A civil servant in the Ministry of Education, the father spoke politics all the time to his seven children, the girls as well as the boys. But his words were never to leave their four walls, so as not to arouse the suspicion of the regime and get them arrested. The discussions around the dinner table forged the views and the future activism of Imad.

When Hama was crushed by the army in February 1982, Imad was in his last year at school. Thirty-eight days after the massacre, the schoolboy, without a word to anyone, decided to go into the town, which the authorities had placed off limits to anyone 'without good reason'. He told his parents he was going to see a friend. To this day, his father is unaware of this. Imad bought a ticket for Aleppo, and the bus had to pass through Hama.

When the bus drove through the streets of the martyred town, everyone looked in frozen horror at the destruction. The man sitting next to Imad covered his face with the keffiyeh that he had wrapped around his head and wept. 'Crying fit to burst', Imad says today. 'He didn't stop for an hour. No one on the bus dared say a word. We shared our sorrow through tears.' Charismatic, calm and gentle, Imad is the sort of man who is not ashamed to cry.

After their meeting, Hassan and Imad would walk together side by side during the years of dictatorship and repression. Together they would help bring about the Syrian National Movement.

Inspired by religious principles, the Syrian National Movement is an umbrella movement incorporating a diversity of groups and tendencies, both Islamist and secular. Unlike the Muslim Brotherhood, whom they regard as rivals, the leaders of the Syrian National Movement are very familiar with the realities of the country. Some members of the organization still live in Syria. And those who are in exile left fairly recently, like Hassan and Imad. Together the two men would take Caesar's file to the international community. They were also linked in their private lives, when the son of one married the daughter of the other.

Before exile, the two activists had undertaken some fieldwork to help the families of prisoners. In his neighbourhood, when Hassan learned that people had disappeared he made discreet confidential inquiries among acquaintances and neighbours: 'Do you know anyone who could give any information on so-and-so? Or anyone with any info on this detention centre?' Painstaking, secret work to draw up lists of 'disappeared', a risky gamble, as you might end up asking the 'wrong' person. These matters always had to be broached in a cautious, subtle manner.

Before approaching a member of the regime, you had to read his thoughts, examine the nature of his links with the authorities. 'In the time of Hafez, the father', Hassan Shalabi posits in our conversation, 'most state officials were there for ideological reasons. In the case of the son, Bashar, many are there simply to make a living. The latter are easier to bribe in return for information. But make no mistake: attempting to corrupt a partisan of the regime can land you in prison alongside the person you were trying to set free!

On several occasions, aided by rich Syrians living abroad, Hassan had managed to free detainees for a fee.

Tell the World

'Imad, come here. I can't talk to you over the phone.' In late autumn 2013, faced with the collection of photos in what would henceforth be known as the 'Caesar file', Hassan realized their full impact. Up until now he had only received a few copies. Gathered together in their thousands, the files took on a whole new dimension. After a 'nightmare night', Hassan decided to show the whole file to Imad Eddine al-Rachid, his travelling companion. For months, the two activists from the Syrian National Movement had been engaged in peaceful opposition to the regime. In September 2011, they and a few others had jointly set up the Syrian National Council, the principal political representation of the forces opposing the regime of Bashar al-Assad.

Imad Eddine al-Rachid rejoined Hassan in this country bordering Syria. He knew of the existence of these photos of prisoners who had died in the detention centres. One of his friends, a businessman, had told him how, for a payment of 600,000 Syrian pounds (4,000 euros), he received proof of the arrest and death of his brother and his cousin. In the offices of the military police, looking at the photos shown to him by an officer, he had recognized the two bodies with their numbers. The businessman had alerted Imad and asked the opposition to take on the case. But at the time the political activist hadn't grasped the full scale of the issue.

Now, faced with all the images together, Imad, like Hassan, would find the revelation shattering. 'I had seen prisoners die and I myself had been arrested and tortured in the 1980s. But I had never seen this. This was organized, systematic killing.' Imad didn't sleep for a week. The ghosts of the dead passed before his eyes every night. Only leaving the light on allowed him to get any rest.

Caesar's file was explosive. Should they pass it on to a human rights organization, hand it over to the United Nations? Did the Syrian National Movement have broad enough shoulders to bring it before the international community? 'We thought of this file as a deposit, it was the file of Syrian blood and it didn't belong to us', Hassan Shalabi explains. 'We felt that we had two responsibilities. First, the families needed to know if their loved ones were on these photos, and thus dead, and second, it was important that they obtained justice.' Imad and Hassan decided to keep the file in the hands of the Syrian National Movement.

That would be their strength and their weakness. Opponents accused them later of trying to take advantage to advance their movement politically. But the two men had been involved in clandestine work for years and they knew that certain opposition groups were exploited and others infiltrated by agents of the regime. They were afraid of being used.

Even within the movement, Imad, Hassan and Sami would spend a certain amount of time working in secret. Their first task was to order and classify the thousands of photos and documents, get an overview so that they could decide what would be divulged to the public, to Western governments, to the legal authorities.

Caesar's exfiltrated file contained three categories of around 53,000 photos.

The first consisted of photos of dead prisoners in the detention centres of the intelligence services or the prisons. The prisoners bore three numbers, including that of the branch of the intelligence services where they were held.

The second was of soldiers of the regime who had been shot dead, apparently in combat. The bodies of the soldiers bore their surname and first name, to which was often appended the word 'martyr'.

Finally, the third category was of civilians, sometimes entire families, men, women, children, grandparents, stretched out on the ground, mostly in their own houses or at the mortuary. Killed by a bullet, blown up by a hand grenade or car bomb, the bodies bore only a single number, occasionally a name.

For two years, between 2011 and 2013, Caesar had copied all the work his service did on a daily basis. Following orders: one morning, the photographers would go to the hospital in Mezzeh to take some pictures of bodies of detainees. The next day they might be sent out into town to photograph the bodies of families. The following day they would go to record the bodies of soldiers killed in an assault or simply in a road accident.

Where Do the Bodies Come From?

Imran, Zakaria
To set the ball rolling, the Syrian National Movement decided to prioritize the photos of the detainees. Their estimate of the number of pictures essentially of dead detainees, given to the media and to governments, was 55,000, which as it happens was wrong. These tens of thousands of photographs contain all three categories: detainees, soldiers of the regime and civilians who had died outside prison. The figure of 55,000 photos of 11,000 prisoners who died in detention would be picked up by the media and the lawyers.

Imad and Hassan set aside the approximately 24,500 photos of 1,036 soldiers and 4,025 civilian victims outside prison in order to concentrate on the photos of the detainees.

In an apartment in Istanbul, not far from Ataturk airport, where the movement had set up its offices, Sami waded through the files every night. He had forgone sleep for a long time. Photo after photo, he recorded the numbers of the dead bodies. Sometimes the image was blurred and the number on the body was hard to read. The former construction engineer had become a forensics archivist.

He listed 26,948 pictures of 6,627 detainees who were imprisoned in twenty-four detention centres located in Damascus.[1] Each detainee was photographed four times by the military photographers.

Most of the prisoners came from Branches 215 and 227 of the military intelligence services.

The figures break down as follows:

- 3,452 were locked up in Branch 215 of the military intelligence services, i.e. 52.09% of the total;

---

1 The list of these centres can be found in Appendix 5.

- 1,998 in Branch 227 of the military intelligence services, i.e. 30.15%;
- 350 in the branch of Air Force Intelligence, i.e. 5.28%;
- 278 in Branch 216 of the military intelligence services, i.e. 4.19%;
- 112 in Branch 235 of the military intelligence services, i.e. 1.69%;
- 99 in Branch 251 of the military intelligence services, i.e. 1.49%;
- 54 in Branch 248 of the military intelligence services, i.e. 0.81%;
- 49 in Branch 220 of the military intelligence services, i.e. 0.74%;
- 45 in the military police, i.e. 0.68%;
- 116 from an unnamed branch, i.e. 1.75%;
- 74 from various services, i.e. 1.12%.

In Syria, in a climate of war and fear, the pictures were copied and recorded hurriedly onto a hard drive. Here, in the calm of the office, they had to rename the photos with the number of the detainee, then arrange them by branches and by date of death. The idea was that it would be easy to access any photo with one click of the mouse. Even if you didn't know the identity of any of the victims.

With the same utmost discretion, Imran, a young IT technician from Mouadamiye, in the suburbs of Damascus, joined Sami in his work. Wanted by the regime, he had left the country, like thousands of other activists who abandoned jobs, homes and, frequently, family and started a new life elsewhere. A secret life for those, and there are many of them, who continued their militant activities. They continued to introduce themselves using their resistance name in order to protect those they left behind from the attentions of the security services.

Imran passed through Egypt before arriving in Tunisia. Imad Eddine al-Rachid, who knew him, entrusted to him the task of reorganizing the file. Imran had nowhere to stay, he slept in offices of the Syrian National Movement. At twenty-six years old, he was still a boy. Alone with the faces immortalized by Caesar's team, he discovered horror.

'Seeing all these images back then made me depressed. I started hating everyone', Imran tells me. 'It was as if I had no feelings any more, as if the angel of death[2] were coming to claim my soul.' Imran's only therapy was forgetting, and so he has already lost some of his memories. The rooms of the house he grew up in, his school friends. The details of certain dramatic events.

Like that morning in Syria when the whole family assembled in one of the mosques of Mouadamiye to bid farewell to one of their cousins killed at a roadblock by regime militia. A car bomb went off in front of the place of worship. As the windows shattered into pieces, Imran, in a state of shock, got up and ran towards his car to go to the hospital, as if he were on his own. Then, remembering that he had left his family behind him in the mosque, he retraced his steps and found the building destroyed and body parts scattered among the rubble. His parents and cousins were wounded but being cared for, but the trauma remained. The family came to bury a young man that morning. By the evening, there were thirty-seven others to bury.

'Today, my memory fails me', the young man recognizes. 'I have trouble concentrating, learning.' How do you escape unscathed from the sight of 27,000 photographs of inhumanity?

Soon they would be joined by another activist. Going under the pseudonym of Zakaria, this former

2 The servant of God for Muslims.

paediatrician from Damascus arrived from Lebanon, where he had first sought refuge. Imad Eddine al-Rachid was aware of his particular expertise and appealed to him for help: 'You are a doctor. What can you derive from these photos? Could you, for example, create a list of the tortures these people had to endure?'

Zakaria agreed to create a second Excel spreadsheet. For several weeks he sat in front of his computer, scrolling through the images, making handwritten notes onto a sheet of paper next to him. In the beginning the doctor worked in stretches of ten minutes at a time. He would be overcome by anger and would have to stand up and walk around, so that it wouldn't solidify into hatred. 'These photos are like a reservoir for the fighters of Islamic State', he argues today. He is also thinking of his three young daughters, who joined him in Turkey with their mother. What can he tell them? 'It's as if they didn't have any history. We won't be returning to Syria any time soon. Where is the school that I could point to and say: "That's where I studied"? I lived in a socially diverse community. Where is it now? My Alawite friends, my Christian schoolteacher … Where are they? The mosaic that was Syria no longer exists.'

'I left Syria as if on a moonless night, without saying farewell to my mother or kissing her goodbye.' An activist had warned him by phone as he arrived at hospital, where he was about to go on duty: 'You should leave the country right now.' Zakaria went to a friend's house, borrowed his mobile and alerted his wife, who brought him his passport the following day. He destroyed his SIM card and removed the batteries from his phone. Another activist checked that his name was not flagged up at the border posts, and he went to Lebanon. 'Three days later, members of the intelligence services came to look for me at the hospital. Too late.'

Sitting in front of his computer in Turkey, he tried not to think too much, tried not to linger over the photos. But some of them grabbed his attention. The expression on a man's face, staring at him, almost as if he were still alive, the one screaming in pain, his mouth wide open, as death took him. Zakaria felt close to them and he cried. Then above all there were those who smiled at the moment of death, which to his surprise he found calming.

Inevitably, one day the doctor came across the photo he had been dreading, the one of a teacher who was a member of his activist group, a friend he and Imad had in common. 'He was a hardliner', Zakaria tells me. 'He received threats and should have left Syria, but decided to stay.' Every night, when the activists gathered in cramped rooms to talk about freedom or to organize demonstrations, the teacher placed his laptop on his well-rounded belly, as though on a tray, and started guffawing. 'This is my office.' In the end he was arrested. For a long time, Zakaria and the teacher's family tried to get him released, forking out hundreds of thousands of Syrian pounds. But the negotiations with members of the regime dragged on. In the end, too long.

From the moment he started work on Caesar's file, Zakaria was thinking about him. He came across his photo less than a week later. He was 99 per cent sure that the corpse was that of his friend. Later, when he was working with Imad, he showed him the photo among a pile of others, without saying anything. When he saw Imad look at the picture he knew he hadn't been mistaken. Their friend had indeed died under torture in Branch 215 of military intelligence.

Numbers and Questions

Along with Imran, Zakaria drew up twenty-four criteria to describe the 27,000 pictures of dead prisoners:[3]

- minors, young people under eighteen
- adults
- people over fifty
- emaciation
- skin lesions (due to a lack of hygiene and medical care or the lice, bugs and fleas with which the cells were infested)
- light torture
- use of chemicals
- eyes gouged out
- wounds
- tattoos (some had a cross, others the land of Palestine marked on them; others, Shiites or Alawites, had a sword of Ali on their flesh. One even had the face of Bashar al-Assad covering his chest)
- strangulation
- electric shocks
- severe torture (deep lesions)
- whip marks
- conclusive wounds
- traces of fresh blood (certain detainees had evidently just died, in the hospital itself or on the floor of this garage where the bodies were deposited)
- herniated intestine
- abdomen cut open
- broken limbs
- splints
- holes in the body

---

3 The document can be seen in Appendix 6.

- *tashahhud* (right index finger raised in a sign of faith)
- surgery
- physical disability

One of the 27,000 pictures was not classified in this table. For reasons no doubt of modesty, as she was the only woman in the whole file. Rehab Alallawi was a twenty-four-year-old student in her third year of a civil engineering course at the University of Damascus. Arrested in January 2013 after taking part in demonstrations, dead shortly afterwards and recognizable in her black clothing among all the other bodies photographed.

'The seventy-five detainees who died raising their finger in a sign of allegiance to Islam prove that they saw death coming', Zakaria explains. 'They made the profession of faith because they knew they were going to die. How did they know? Probably the agents interrogating them made it clear to them that their end was near ... The holes in the skin were gunshot wounds, or more rarely wounds made by a drill. Here, we had never come across this type of torture with a drill. This was common practice in Iraqi prisons in the 2000s. Had Iraqi Shiite militia come to Syria to advise the regime or to participate in the repression?'

In the end, the two archivists revised the number of dead victims upwards, counting an extra 6,786. And they included only those who were clearly identifiable. Sometimes only a chest was evident on a photo. Did it belong to someone already accounted for? They decided not to add it to their list.

In December 2015, the organization Human Rights Watch, which gathered together all the images, verified the total number of photos and gave the figure as 53,275, of which 28,707 were of people who had died in detention. Human Rights Watch published an eighty-six-page report entitled 'If the Dead Could Speak: Mass Deaths and Torture in Syria's Detention Facilities'.[4]

Zakaria's Excel spreadsheet showed, among other things, that 2,936 victims had suffered starvation, 2,769 torture and 1,510 wounds to the flesh. Thirty-seven detainees had had their faces or bodies disfigured by a chemical substance. Of these, twelve were held in Branch 215 of the military intelligence services. They died in February 2013 and bore consecutive numbers: 3831, 3832, 3833, 3834, 3835 (this man had electrodes attached to his chest), 3836, 3837, 3838 (this one's body was laid on blue nylon hospital sheet, and on this photo, next to him, you could see the legs of an agent of the regime with yellow boots on his feet), 3839 (this person's body had melted), 3840, 3841 and 3842.

Then there were the 455 detainees who had had their eyes gouged out, 189 of them in Branch 215 alone. The spreadsheet shows several cases in 2012 and early 2013, then, all of a sudden, the figures proliferate, and there are waves of ten, twenty, thirty numbers in succession of detainees whose eyes have been gouged out. For example, the photos taken on 1 June 2013 in the garages of Mezzeh hospital show forty bodies without eyes. On 7 July 2013, there were fifty-seven.

Why? How? Most of the eyes had clearly been removed with a sharp instrument; others had perhaps been eaten by animals roaming the hospital grounds, where the corpses had been left lying for several days. 'When you look at the sequence of numbers of detainees who had had their eyes gouged out', Zakaria expounds, 'you have to come to the conclusion that the members

---

4   https://www.hrw.org/report/2015/12/16/if-dead-could-speak/mass-deaths-and-torture-syrias-detention-facilities.

of the regime just decided one day to mutilate these people one after the other.'

The spreadsheet is incomplete. There are photos missing and numbers missing. Occasionally, two bodies bear the same detainee number. 'Despite the regime's best attempts at establishing a routine, it was not always professional, and its agents could make mistakes', Zakaria explains. 'Many didn't know how to use a computer, and the medical examiner made handwritten notes … Also, Caesar copied these photos under stressful circumstances, which might have caused him to forget certain files recorded on the computer at the office of the military police.'

One thing is for certain: the file contains head-spinning sequences of numbers. As well as the torture, overcrowding of cells, starvation, decoding these numbers is to decipher the Syrian death machine, its workings, its mechanism.

To reiterate, each photographed body bore three numbers: two – written on the skin or on a strip of white adhesive tape – with the detainee's individual number and that of the branch in whose custody he was. The medical examiner then added a third, which he wrote on a sheet of paper or a piece of white cardboard, which was placed on the body at the moment the photo was taken.

The numbers given by the doctor are clear. They are in sequence because the doctor wrote down the numbers in his notebook one after the other: 1 to 5,000. He then moved on to a new series: 1/b, 2/b, 3/b … up to 5,000b, then a third series, 1/th, 2/th, 3/th … Why does this series not have the third letter of the Arabic alphabet, *t*, but instead the fourth, *th*? No one knows. And why does each series stop at 5,000? Simply how the system worked, probably.

The detainees' individual numbers are more complicated to decipher. Was it a number given by the agents when the prisoner died and was taken out of the cell? The regime would then simply number the bodies as and when they died, whatever the cause of death: starvation, disease, strangulation, torture.

Or does the number correspond to the file on the person arrested when he was first taken into detention? The soldiers – or, more likely, other detainees delegated to do it – would then take this number from the file and write it on the body. This hypothesis then raises another: the serial execution of detainees who bore successive numbers. 'One can imagine the head of a detention centre making such a decision', Zakaria conjectures. 'One day he might say: "Give me the list of detainees, and kill all those between numbers X and Y." That would be even more terrifying. But we don't know for certain. We haven't found this out yet, or obtained any evidence.

'The system is compartmentalized', he continues. 'Each agent, each officer carries out his work in ignorance of what is happening in the office next door. Caesar had to go to the hospital to photograph the bodies and then return to the office to archive his files. That's it. He never went inside a detention centre or a hospital. The head of a detention centre might even have less power or be less in the loop than one of his subordinates, if the latter has some link to the Assad family. An order from a chief might not be carried out by an inferior who is close to the president.'

Hamza al-Khatib, Aged Thirteen, Is There ...

In Istanbul, in the office of the Syrian National Movement, Zakaria the doctor became a teacher, Zakaria the dissident explained his war. Applying an academic exactitude to his memories, he used a felt-tip pen to sketch out the bodies on a whiteboard, drawing circles to represent the cells, adding in the numbers and noting the question marks. A lot of question marks. Then the regrets hit him again: that of having left his country, his house, the Revolution. 'Activism inside Syria is not the same as that on the outside.' He had never seen himself as an activist, just as he never imagined himself spending his nights archiving photos of dead bodies.

When revolution broke out in Tunisia and Egypt, Zakaria did not think that conditions were rife for something similar in his own country, but he realized it was now or never. 'It was like a wave sweeping you along. We enjoyed going out demonstrating, shouting slogans. I don't know where we found the courage. We learned to take off our leather shoes and put on trainers or espadrilles to make it easier to run during rallies.'

On 29 April 2011, a month after the start of the Revolution, was young Hamza al-Khatib running to avoid arrest? This chubby thirteen-year-old boy with the broad smile on his identity photo became an icon of the Syrian Revolution in the same way that Mohammed Bouazizi, the Tunisian who burned himself to death, initiating the Arab Spring, or Khaled Said, who was tortured to death in Alexandria, Egypt, became for theirs.

This particular morning, Hamza left his small village with his family and friends to go on a demonstration in Deraa, in the south of the country, which was at the forefront of the peaceful revolution. Syrian online activists dubbed this Friday 'The day we end the siege of Deraa'. This major town was indeed encircled by the army.

But Hamza didn't even reach the outskirts. About ten kilometres outside the town, some soldiers stopped them at a roadblock. His body was returned to his parents a month later. Bullet wounds in his arms, his penis cut off, his face bloated. His body blue with haematoma. His family immediately posted a video of his mutilated body on the internet. His name was chanted at rallies, his picture was paraded. People set up Facebook pages and web pages dedicated to him.

The regime gave its own version of events on a state TV channel: Hamza al-Khatib was a young man swayed by calls to jihad and died while participating in an attack against the officers' quarters in Saida in order to rape their wives. A medical report published on 1 June even stated that 'the body showed no traces of torture, contusions or violence'. According to a medical examiner cited in this report, the visible marks were due to the decomposition of the body, the authorities having been unable to quickly identify the boy. 'The report definitively debunks the lies and allegations and shows the truth', claimed the official press agency Sana.

Three years later, Caesar's photos offered proof that the teenager had been tortured by the intelligence services: the photo of his body was one of hundreds of pictures of murdered civilians classified as 'terrorists' by the regime. Hamza al-Khatib's body bore the number 23.

Another photo showed the body of Thamer al-Sharei. A fifteen-year-old boy, arrested in Deraa the same day as Hamza, whose body, riddled with eleven bullet wounds and with a large cut on his cheek, was returned to his family two months later. Thamer's photo bears the number 12.

These photos of children in Deraa confirmed that photos of civilians were taken in detention centres outside Damascus then ordered and archived centrally by Caesar's team within the military police. Photos resembling those taken of Hamza al-Khatib and Thamer al-Sharei. The two boys were well known and, thanks to their archived photos, instantly recognized.

But the others? Who were they? Such as that family completely decimated in 2012. In the photos, their bodies are laid out on a white tiled floor, speckled with black marks, inside a house. They bear the same number twice: on a strip of white tape stuck to their skin and on a wooden card laid on their bodies.

There were two teenagers who seemed to have been shot in the head; they bore the numbers 4 and 29. A woman, with the back of her skull ripped off, and number 18 laid on her dress, lay next to another woman, who had stretched out her arm towards her and bore the number 19. And an old man. The man was laid out straight in an almost dignified posture. He was naked apart from some incontinence pants. He had a piece of tape on his chest and a piece of wood on his leg, both bearing the number 9.

'How did these people become anonymous numbers? These victims should get their identities back. Their family has a right to know what happened to them.' On this December day in 2014, that is, a year and a half after Caesar's escape, Zakaria is bitter. He doesn't understand. Why doesn't the world act? What are the politicians and the international community doing? 'We thought that our work would mobilize public opinion. The photos have been shown to the European Union, the US Congress in Washington, the United Nations Human Rights Council. But the politicians want to let bygones be bygones and negotiate with Bashar al-Assad. How did we get to this point?'

9
The Failure of
Gradual Diplomacy

Over the course of a few months, before he stepped back from the matter in late 2014 for personal reasons, Hassan Shalabi, the man with 'executive responsibility', as he liked to put it himself, along with Imad Eddine al-Rachid, the 'politician' of the group, showed the Caesar file around in various diplomatic and legal circles.

In late 2013, while Sami and Imran were archiving the photos in Istanbul, Imad and Hassan were showing the photos to small groups, testing the reaction of experts in informal meetings, establishing contacts with international lawyers. The Qatari minister quickly came to the conclusion that the Syrian National Movement should receive financial support. When he saw the twenty or so pictures spread out on his desk, Khaled al-Attiyah looked away and warned: 'We have to put these criminals on trial. If we do nothing, history will be our judge.'

A few weeks later, in Paris, the stunned reaction of Laurent Fabius and the ten other foreign ministers of the Core Group of the Friends of Syria to the video which unveiled the dossier finally convinced Imad Eddine al-Rachid: the photos provided compelling evidence of the terrorism of the Syrian state.

So Imad Eddine al-Rachid set off for Switzerland in a confident mood. The negotiations between factions of the opposition and the regime were due to open in Montreux on 22 January and then continue in Geneva. He was sure that the Geneva 2 conference would provide a good forum. To increase the impact of the photos on the negotiators, the opposition exclusively revealed their existence to the *Guardian* newspaper in the UK and the US rolling news channel CNN. The two media companies posted a few of the photos on their websites, as well as the full text of the consultant's report by Carter-Ruck and Co., which stated that 'the inquiry team found him [Caesar], for its part, to be a truthful and credible witness. ... Although he was a supporter of those who opposed the present regime, the inquiry team is satisfied that he gave an honest account of his experiences. If he wished to exaggerate his evidence it would have been very easy for him to say that he had actually witnessed executions [of detainees]. ... There were many other reasons which drove the inquiry team to its conclusion that his evidence was reliable and could safely be acted upon in any subsequent judicial proceedings.'[1]

CNN flagged up the 'systematic torture and killing' of the Assad regime and interviewed, among others, Desmond de Silva, who had headed up the team of experts. The former prosecutor of the Special Court for Sierra Leone acknowledged that his team had approached his work with 'a certain amount of scepticism', but that the images of bodies of detainees who had starved to death that they had seen 'are

---

1 https://www.carter-ruck.com/images/uploads/documents/ Syria_Report-January_2014.pdf.

reminiscent of the pictures of those [who] were found still alive in the Nazi death camps after World War II. ... This evidence could underpin a charge of crimes against humanity – without any shadow of a doubt. ... Of course it's not for us to make a decision. All we can do is evaluate the evidence and say this evidence is capable of being accepted by a tribunal as genuine.'²

At the negotiating table of the Geneva 2 peace talks on 22 January, Ahmad Jarba, president of the Syrian National Coalition, waved one of the photos under the nose of the representatives of the regime. In the picture several naked, emaciated bodies were laid out side by side, having apparently died of starvation. Ahmad Jarba demanded the resignation of Bashar al-Assad and the dismantling of the security services, which were responsible for the repression. Sitting opposite, the Damascus contingent was quick to denounce the partisan influence of Qatar behind this report. Moscow, which unconditionally supported the Syrian regime, demanded that the allegations be verified. Since the start of the Revolution and the war, Russia had refused to voice the slightest criticism of the regime, which had been an ally for decades and its seventh most important customer in terms of arms sales, and which offered them access to the Mediterranean via a naval base at Tartus, at which its ships could dock.

A year later, in January 2015, in a long interview with the American magazine *Foreign Affairs*, President Bashar al-Assad reiterated his criticism of the report. In one question, the journalist referred to the accusations of 'indiscriminate bombing of civilian targets,

---

2 'Gruesome Syria photos may prove torture by Assad regime', CNN, 3 February 2015, available at: http://edition.cnn.com/2014/01/20/world/syria-torture-photos-amanpour/index.html, accessed 18 July 2017.

photo evidence provided by the defector code-named Caesar [...] showing terrible torture and abuse in Syrian prisons'.

The Syrian president replied:

'Who took these pictures? Who is he? Nobody knows. There is no verification of any of this evidence, so it's all allegations without evidence.'

'But Caesar's photos have been looked at by independent European investigators', the journalist insisted.

'No, no. It's funded by Qatar, and they say it's an anonymous source. So nothing is clear or proven. The pictures are not clear which person they show. They're just pictures of a head, for example, with some skulls. Who said this is done by the government, not by the rebels? Who said this is a Syrian victim, not someone else? For example, photos published at the beginning of the crisis were from Iraq and Yemen ...'[3]

Dashed Hopes

Around the time of Geneva 2, 'we had high hopes', Imad Eddine al-Rachid recalls. 'We knew the photos wouldn't bring down Bashar al-Assad, because the conflict has become very complicated, with Russia and Iran propping up the regime. But we thought that this damning evidence would help us, that it would prick consciences and influence the direction of the negotiations.'

The French newspaper *Le Monde*, which was covering the talks, published an opening article on 'the defection

---

3 Interview with President Bashar al-Assad, *Foreign Affairs*, 26 January 2015, available at: https://www.foreignaffairs. com/interviews/2015-01-25/syrias-president-speaks.

of Caesar, photographer of Syrian barbarity'. Caesar's story did the rounds of the Western media.

In Paris, the initial reaction of certain intellectuals and researchers who worked on Syria was one of relief. 'Finally! Something that will reveal the full scale of the horror', recalls Bassma Kodmani, the director of the research centre Arab Reform Initiative. This Franco-Syrian political researcher was the mouthpiece for the Syrian National Council. Thinking that it lacked credibility, she was obliged to leave the organization eight months later to devote herself to humanitarian work on behalf of the Syrian people. 'We were relieved that someone was exposing these horrors that no one was seeing in the full light of day', she goes on. 'We all had so many friends who had died in prison, we knew that they were places of death, but not like this … we were surprised ourselves by these numbers, this documentation, these systematic photographs. This meticulous care in recording everything. Beyond a certain point, horror becomes indescribable. We need facts, images to do the talking, because no one can find the words to describe such barbarism.'

But the talks between the opposition and the regime ended in failure. Damascus refused to contemplate any sort of political transition, and presented itself as a bulwark against Islamic State terrorism. In the following weeks, Caesar disappeared from the media, rendered invisible by the demands of realpolitik. Too many images of dead Syrians on all sides in the media. Henceforth, the barbarism of the jihadists would overshadow the ongoing suffering of the civilian population under the regime's repression. Public opinion, grown weary, had come to the conclusion that the conflict had become 'incomprehensible'. Very few diplomats properly took on board Caesar's file.

Five months after having refused to strike against the regime for its responsibility for the chemical attack on Ghouta in the suburbs of Damascus, Washington stuck to its political line: toppling Bashar al-Assad was not the top priority.

The Americans had fresh memories of their recent experiences in Iraq in 2003. In trying to rebuild the political system from scratch, they created a state of chaos which facilitated the emergence of Islamic State. So now the main issue was containing the lightning advance of the jihadists in Iraq and Syria. Even if it meant leaving Bashar al-Assad and the members of his regime in power. And so it became a truism that if the president was removed from power, the situation that followed would be much worse.

Above all, America wanted to disengage from the Middle East. They had done this in Iraq when they pulled their troops out. And now they wanted to achieve a settlement with Iran.

In the face of this political inertia, a handful of intellectuals met in Paris in late winter 2014 to attempt to relaunch the Caesar file. Among them were Bassma Kodmani, Ziad Majed and Yassin Al-Haj Saleh.

A political analyst specializing in democratic transitions in the Arab world, Ziad Majed[4] had experienced the Lebanese civil war and had shared the pain of civilians while working with the Red Cross. He currently teaches at the American University in Paris.

A Syrian doctor and author, Yassin Al-Haj Saleh[5] himself spent more than sixteen years in regime

---

4   Ziad Majed, *Syrie. La Révolution orpheline* [Syria. The Orphan Revolution] (Actes Sud, 2014).
5   Yassin Al-Haj Saleh, *Récits d'une Syrie oubliée. Sortir la mémoire des prisons* [Stories from Forgotten Syria. Releasing Prison Memories] (Les Prairies ordinaires, 2015).

prisons between 1980 and 1997. After the start of the Revolution, he spent two and a half years in hiding before being forced to flee the country at the end of 2013 to seek refuge in Turkey. His brother Firas was abducted by Islamic State militia in his native town of Raqqa in summer 2013, and his wife, Samira Khalil, an activist and former political prisoner, was abducted in a suburb of Damascus in December 2013, probably by an Islamic group (Jaysh al-Islam, Army of Islam).

Samira Khalil was with three other activists at the time. (As of summer 2015, they still haven't been found.) Among them was the lawyer Razan Zaitouneh, a famous champion of human rights over many years, who founded the Violations Documentation Centre in April 2011 and the Local Coordination Committees of Syria in June 2011. The centre started by establishing a list of victims of the suppression of demonstrations. Then it set about identifying civilians killed in bombing raids and those who had disappeared or been detained by the regime or kidnapped or killed by Islamic State. This was essential work which would one day allow proper remembrance.

In Paris that evening, everyone was uneasy about the silence that surrounded the Caesar file. 'The fact that it wasn't taken up at a judicial level made it feel as if the Syrians had been expelled from the international order', according to Bassma Kodmani. 'They are placed outside the law and told: "You have no rights. Assad has taken them away from you. You will have no access to justice to restore those rights." That is disastrous, as the victims might turn into monsters unless norms of right and wrong are re-established.'

'We didn't understand how such a dossier could pass under the radar', Ziad Majed explains. 'The numbers on the bodies show the scale of the systematic repression on the part of the regime. But there needed to be a political will to take the file forward. We decided to try something in France.' Yassin Al-Haj Saleh published a forum on lexpress.fr, 'The Murder Industry in Syria':[6] 'What is going on in other Syrian cities: Aleppo, Homs, Latakia, Deir ez-Zor, etc.? We don't know, but there is no reason to assume that the murders committed against prisoners of the regime are confined to Damascus. The macabre bookkeeping of victims of torture and the photographs we have in our possession reveal the existence of a murder industry.'

The Caesar File in Paris

Following their get-together, this group of intellectuals suggested three meetings, to be organized by the Network of Syrian Women and the Syrian Association for the Disappeared and Prisoners of Conscience. At the European Parliament in Strasbourg, at the Institute of the Arab World in Paris and at Amnesty International. Amnesty saw Caesar's file as confirmation of their various reports, such as the one published two years earlier, 'I Wanted to Die'.[7] On the morning of 13 March 2014, the human rights organization warmly welcomed the group that had exfiltrated Caesar in Paris, as well as David Crane, one of the legal experts who wrote the report.

Imad Eddine al-Rachid and Hassan Shalabi described the operation in detail. David Crane authenticated the photos. A Syrian doctor based in Bordeaux, Chadi Joneib, spoke on behalf of the Syrian Association for the Disappeared and Prisoners of Conscience. This

---

6 http://www.lexpress.fr/actualite/l-industrie-du-meutre-en-syrie_1499834.html.
7 https://www.amnestyusa.org/files/mde24016201 2en.pdf, accessed 18 July 2017.

organization was in the process of setting itself up to help families find their missing loved ones who had disappeared between spring 2011 and summer 2013, the period in which the photos in the file had been taken. Using photos and other information provided by the families, members of the association would check to see if the photo matched any of the pictures in Caesar's file.

'I always knew that the regime was pitiless and that it tortured prisoners', Chadi Joneib, a refugee in France with his family since he was young, would say later. 'When we were children, our parents spoke to us about it. When we returned to Syria, we were always afraid of being arrested at Damascus airport and being disappeared. We had read *Al-Qawqa'a* [The Shell] by Mustafa Khalife,[8] but, to be honest, we thought the book fictionalized the issue somewhat. I understood once I saw the photos.'

The author of *Al-Qawqa'a* was also at this meeting. The book, in which he described his thirteen years in the prison at Palmyra, from 1981 to 1994, has become a touchstone. Also exiled in France, Mustafa Khalife reaffirmed that the repression did not begin with the Revolution, but is one of the underlying principles of the regime. 'But with one major difference, and that is the level of repression. At the time of the father, Hafez al-Assad, many prisoners died under torture. But death was not the aim. If the prisoner died under torture, it wasn't too serious. The aim was to obtain as much information as possible and to humiliate the prisoners. Today there is a difference: in many cases, in the prisons of the son, Bashar al-Assad, the aim is simply to kill.'

The former prisoner of conscience questioned the 'inaction' of those in diplomatic circles who justified

---

8   *Al-Qawqa'a* [The Shell] (Beirut: Dar al-Adab, 2008).

themselves by expressing fears about the breakdown of the Syrian state and the chaos that would result. 'But is there really a Syrian state in the modern sense of the word? A judicial and political structure, a form of social contract within a society as a way of organizing the lives, interests and the protection of its citizens. No, Assad runs Syria like he would run a farm, a private property, where the feudal lord possesses both the land and his subjects. So there is no real state in Syria to break down.'

The conference came to an end, the journalists dispersed. Then a man arrived, discreetly, who knew Syria well. A former doctor turned diplomat, he was known for his plain speaking and love of field work. Appointed French ambassador to Damascus in spring 2009, Eric Chevallier was in the post when the Revolution broke out. On 7 and 8 July 2011, with his American counterpart, he went to Hama, where thousands of Syrians were protesting.

At the time, the diplomat had already warned the French government that the Bashar regime would not easily be toppled, but in Paris everyone was banking on a rapid fall. In the face of state repression, Nicolas Sarkozy, the French president, decided to close the French embassy in Damascus. So Eric Chevallier left Syria on 6 March 2012. He would continue his work based in the French capital. He built up his contacts with the opposition in exile and with humanitarian NGOs, even going as far as transporting suitcases of banknotes to the Turkish–Syrian border to aid local councils in liberated villages, who were trying to replace the institutions of the regime.

Like the other members of the French government, Eric first heard about the Caesar file in January 2014, when the Friends of the Syrian People met at the Foreign Ministry in Paris. In March, he took advantage of a visit by Caesar's group to France to set up discussions with them. 'At the ministry, we knew that an international team of magistrates and experts in legal medicine had done work on the file and that it was serious', he explains. So the French ambassador to Syria accompanied Imad Eddine al-Rachid, Hassan Shalabi and David Crane to the Quai d'Orsay for a working meeting. There were a dozen people there: a representative of the president, a representative of the Crisis Centre, senior members of the United Nations, international and human rights organizations and others from the organization Afrique du Nord et Moyen-Orient, a collaborator of the ambassador of human rights responsible for the international dimension of the Shoah, spoliation and the duty of memory. The discussion covered Caesar's file, terrorism and diplomatic action.

Seven months after the Americans had reneged on their threat to launch air strikes in retaliation for chemical attacks in the suburbs of Damascus, and the inability of Paris to go it alone without American help, the Caesar case offered an opportunity to take the initiative again. And, Eric Chevallier adds, 'to reaffirm the French position, which held that the regime was largely responsible for this conflict. This file is also important for posterity, so that these crimes are not forgotten about.'

The two other meetings involving the Caesar group, organized by the intellectuals, involved specialist audiences. The day before the meeting with Amnesty, on 12 March, a meeting was held in the European Parliament in Strasbourg, at the invitation of the Green MEPs Isabelle Durand and Daniel Cohn-Bendit. Shalabi, Al-Rachid, Khalife and Crane all spoke about 'mass torture' before an audience of around thirty. On the evening of the 13th, the group went to the Institut du monde arabe (Institute of the Arab World). The president of IMA, Jack Lang, opened the conference in person.

Istanbul, Spring 2014

Eric Chevallier decided to go further and meet Caesar in person. With the backing of the French government, he flew to Istanbul, where the former photographer had sought temporary refuge. A dinner was organized at the house of Imad Eddine al-Rachid. Hassan Shalabi was present, along with the French consul and a translator. The ambassador was hoping Caesar would be present, but the clock ticked by, and he didn't show up. Imad Eddine al-Rachid explained to his host that he was afraid and didn't want to see anyone. He had, in fact, just refused to meet Stephen Rapp, the American ambassador responsible for international justice.

So Imad fetched Sami, Caesar's closest friend, who lived nearby. Taciturn, reserved to the point of being defensive, the former civil engineer confirmed that Caesar did not wish to appear in public. Midnight came and went. Sitting in Imad's living room with the others, Eric Chevallier drank cup after cup of tea, patient but embarrassed, an involuntary witness to the tensions that racked the group. How could it have been otherwise?

Caesar had left Syria almost six months earlier, the photos had been authenticated, and nothing had happened. On neither the political nor the judicial front. The defector had moved from one country to another. He was in a fragile psychological state. Cautious, increasingly sceptical, perhaps. Where should he finally settle? Where would he be safest?

The Caesar file offered an image of the Syrian conflict: activists inside the country and political activists outside. Some of these activists have been in exile for many years, virtually cut off from the present-day realities of life in

Syria. Others, who remained rooted in the country, had to flee at the start of the Revolution. Communists, socialists, Islamists, defenders of human rights, they tried to pursue the 'Syrian cause' from Turkey, Jordan, Europe.

In Syria, the activists risk their lives to carry on transmitting information, collecting evidence of crimes, trying to evade both the repression of the regime and the barbarity of Islamic State. The activists on the outside lobby within diplomatic circles forge links through meetings and conferences to take decisions that might stop the conflict. But which decisions?

The first type are a million miles away from the hushed workings of international politics and feel abandoned by the world. The second sort try to carve out a place in this world, often forgetting how dangerous the situation in Syria is.

In Imad's living room that evening in spring 2014, Sami finally rose to his feet and went out onto the balcony to make a phone call. Around one o'clock in the morning, there was a knock at the door. Caesar came in. 'He was in a very anxious state', Eric Chevallier recalls. 'That's understandable. You couldn't have spent so much time living under a regime such as that without knowing what it is capable of.' The meeting was short, but it gave the ambassador confirmation of how vitally important Caesar's file was. Through his caution and vigilance, Chevallier became the first diplomat to meet the defector. The two men would meet again on numerous occasions.

At the Quai d'Orsay, four or five directorates had started to get involved in the case, such as those of the United Nations and Afrique du Nord et Moyen-Orient. How could the case be carried forward politically and judicially? At first, no clear decisions were reached, except to present the file to the Security Council of the UN.

No Referral to the International Criminal Court

New York, April 2014. Gérard Araud, France's ambassador to the United Nations, proposed a meeting of the members of the Security Council according to the 'Arria' protocol, which allows the fifteen members of the council to get together informally. France wanted to avoid a Russian veto at a plenary session in the main meeting room of the council. Three times already since the start of the crisis, this ally of Damascus, and a permanent member of the Security Council, had opposed resolutions condemning Syrian repression and demanding the departure of Bashar al-Assad.

On this 15 April, the fifteen members of the Security Council are all represented, including Russia. Gérard Araud showed the pictures to prepare the ground for a vote on a resolution designed to refer the matter to the International Criminal Court (ICC).

The ICC was created in 2002 to investigate mass crimes (genocides, crimes against humanity, war crimes) in countries where the national authorities refuse to do so. Such countries, however, have to be signatories of the Rome treaty, which had instituted the ICC. One hundred and twenty-two countries have signed up, but not Syria.

When it comes to countries that are not signatories, only the Security Council of the UN can refer cases to the prosecutor of the ICC, who would then be able to investigate, issue arrest warrants and pass judgement on crimes committed in Syria. To refer the case to the ICC, the Security Council had to vote on a resolution in accordance with chapter VII of the United Nations charter.

In an attempt to encourage the Russians to back the draft resolution, France made reference to all the crimes of all parties in the conflict: the regime, but also the opposition fighters, the jihadists ... But France knew that the Security Council was divided and worried that the resolution would not be passed. 'After the decision you make', Gérard Araud declared in the session of 15 April, 'you will have to look yourselves in the mirror ... and you will have to tell yourselves: "What did I do when it was the time?"'[9]

Thirty or so of Caesar's photos were projected, and there followed a few minutes of silence. 'Those who were there that day swore that there had never been a session of the Security Council as moving as that one', a French government spokesperson claims. 'Even the Russian delegate was shocked.'

In the afternoon, Gérard Araud held a press conference.[10] Discussing the forthcoming vote to refer the matter to the ICC, he said: 'We hope that what will speak is not politics, but simply the human conscience ... There are moments when simply the voice of morality must speak out. Moments when we have to appeal to the human conscience. ... This is an opportunity such as we have rarely seen in the history of humanity to decide what we will do in the face of this horror perpetrated by the regime. The International Criminal Court should be able to conduct an inquiry.'

Then the diplomat gave the floor to the two experts who worked on the report by the London law firm Carter-Ruck and Co.: the former prosecutor David Crane and the forensic pathologist attached to the British Home Office, Dr Stuart Hamilton. Visibly moved

---

9 http://www.reuters.com/article/us-syria-crisis-un-idUSBREA3E1RY20140415.

10 http://webtv.un.org/search/the-situation-in-syria-gérard-araud-france-david-m.-crane-scsl-and-dr.-stuart-j.-hamilton-pressconference/3472283372001/?term=araud&sort=date.

but with great restraint, the latter gave a commentary on the twenty-two photos displayed on a giant TV screen.

Photo number 2 showed three bodies laid out on a dirt floor. Also visible were the feet of two people who were standing. 'We have here significant proof of starvation', the forensic expert explained. 'We can see the colour of the bones [under the skin]. The abdomen is sunken and the hip bones are sticking out. On the legs you can even see some of the tendons of the muscles. This is a very severe wasting of the body and in keeping with prolonged starvation.'

On photo number 6, the ankles are marked with broad striations. 'A lot of them showed this marked ulceration around the ankles', Stuart Hamilton explained. 'The precise reason that this has occurred is not 100 per cent clear. I think the most likely explanation is that it is a combination of pressure, most likely from bindings or shackles of some kind, with loss of the strength of the skin as the result of malnutrition. We are all aware of diseases such as scurvy that can appear in people who are malnourished. ... And this is a very common finding among the photos that we examined.'

Describing a photo of a face with its eyes gouged out, the doctor said: 'I haven't seen much like this in my career. And I can think of no innocent or natural explanation as to how someone could come to look like this.' In photo number 12, a hand showed blistering 'entirely in keeping with some sort of chemical burn ... [causing] very severe and clearly painful injuries, but not the sort of injuries you would expect to kill you.'

Photo number 14 showed the hangar where the bodies were laid out before being put into plastic bags. 'As someone who in my day-to-day life deals with transporting bodies from one place to another, wrapping in plastic is certainly a very practical way to make sure they are easy to carry.' The caption on the picture read:

'The way the bodies are accumulated indicates that the process seemed like a production line.'

Finally, in another photo, a detainee seems to have been strangled by the timing belt of a car, which he still had wrapped round his neck.

One month later, on 22 May, at the instigation of France, the UN Security Council was ready to vote on the resolution to refer the case to the International Criminal Court. Before the vote, Gérard Araud warned: 'People are being killed, tortured, raped today in Syria, not only as the terrible consequence of a civil war, but as part of a deliberate political decision to terrorize and punish. ... [The Council] will thus say that in 2014 you cannot act as if we are in 1942 or in 1994, that it cannot allow a return to such barbarity. Perhaps this time we will stop an executioner on the brink of committing a crime.'

That same day, the French minister Laurent Fabius published an op-ed in *Le Monde*. He mentioned chemical weapons, barrel bombs, attacks on civilians, use of sexual violence as a weapon of war and the prisoners of the regime: 'Detainees are tortured in the tens of thousands. International law classifies these atrocities as "war crimes" and "crimes against humanity". If there is a scale of horror, these crimes are among the most serious. To this day, there have been no legal sanctions against those responsible. There have been no convictions. They carry on with complete impunity. Making those responsible for these war crimes and crimes against humanity answerable is the way to give justice to the victims. It is also a means of dissuading those who continue to commit them: sooner or later, they will be judged.'

France was not alone in demanding action from the ICC. In March 2013, in a dialogue session between the Human Rights Council and the UN Special Commission of Inquiry on Syria, sixty-four member states of the United Nations had approved a declaration calling for a referral to the International Criminal Court on the matter of the conflict in Syria. On 15 May 2014, more than one hundred civil society organizations petitioned the fifteen members of the Security Council for just such a referral, to adjudicate on crimes committed by all sides in the conflict.

But on 22 May, the Security Council did not acquiesce to the request contained in the French resolution. Thirteen out of the fifteen nations voted in favour, by raising a hand. The Russians and the Chinese imposed a double veto. The Russian representative called the French text a 'publicity stunt'. Since the start of the crisis, China had not wavered from the principle of non-interference in the affairs of a sovereign state.

A United Nations Impasse

In Geneva, in the other tribunals of the United Nations, there was the same diplomatic impasse. The UN Special Commission of Inquiry on Syria, created in 2011 by the UN High Commission for Human Rights, published a report every six months, detailing all the atrocities committed. Forbidden entry into the country, the investigators of the team headed by the Brazilian Paulo Pinheiro interviewed witnesses in the neighbouring countries. They had already established five lists of those suspected of war crimes and crimes against humanity: leaders of armed opposition groups, military commanders of the regime, heads of branches of intelligence services ... But these lists were confidential and had been languishing for months inside a safe. The commission had always refused to reveal whether Bashar al-Assad or his associates appeared on the lists.

In its eighth report, dated 13 August 2014, the commission referred to the Caesar file without mentioning it by name. Paragraph 26 in the chapter entitled 'Violations relative to the treatment of civilians and *hors de combat* fighters' in fact stipulates: 'A preliminary review and forensic analysis has been conducted of 26,948 photographs allegedly taken between 2011 and 2013 in government detention facilities. Among them are photographs of case files and deceased detainees showing signs of torture and severe malnourishment. Certain elements – such as the location identified in some photographs as Military Hospital No. 601 in Damascus, the methods of torture, and the conditions of detention – support the commission's long-standing findings of systematic torture and deaths of detainees. Investigations are ongoing, with findings largely reliant on the identification of further metadata.'[11]

Only nine lines in the forty-nine pages of the report. The members of the commission met Caesar several times in the different countries where he sought refuge. But the commission refused to confirm this: 'We never reveal our sources. It is a feature of our methodology.' In its subsequent report, published on 5 February 2015, the commission, citing the numerous accounts it had gathered, denounced the 'existence of a state policy implemented across governorates' and 'a system of widespread and systematic torture and unlawful killing'.[12]

These denunciations had no effect, as the case could not be referred to the International Criminal Court. But there was no sign of diplomatic protest. The reports reported, the witnesses bore witness, then … nothing?

---

11 Text available at: http://www.ohchr.org/Documents/ HRBodies/HRCouncil/ColSyria/A.HRC.27.60_Eng.pdf, accessed 7 December 2017.

12 Text available at: http://www.ohchr.org/Documents/ HRBodies/HRCouncil/ColSyria/A.HRC.27.60_Eng.pdf, accessed 7 December 2017.

'I knew that the file would take time', Imad Eddine al-Rachid acknowledges. 'But I am no longer optimistic. I hope that this will lead to legal action, but the main problem derives from the American position vis-à-vis the Syrian conflict.'

In summer 2014, Imad persuaded Caesar to go to Washington to try to convince the Obama administration. Caesar would testify in front of the congressional Foreign Affairs Committee. Dominated by Republicans, who were opposed to the president's policy of non-intervention, the House of Representatives was ready to welcome him. It would be more complicated where the White House was concerned.

10

Testimony in Washington

Caesar

'At first I wondered why I should go. Did the world, the United States, need these photos to know what was going on in Syria? They already knew about the chemical attacks on civilians. The world knows enough about what is going on there to make the decision to intervene in Syria.

'I was unsure, because if the American administration had really wanted to help the Syrian people they would have done so after the major chemical attack on Ghouta, near Damascus.

'I was very afraid of going there for reasons of security. But I agreed to go. I had to speak to members of Congress, to the American people and to the American administration.

'When I arrived at the hotel, Evan McMullin, a member of Congress, greeted me and took charge of my security. He was a good man. I could sense that he wanted to support the Syrian people. He had bought me a baseball cap, some large dark glasses and a blue hoodie which I wore several times to meetings I attended so as not to be identified.

'The day after we arrived, we went first of all to the Holocaust Museum. I was very scared. I was wearing the clothes given to me by the congressman, but the museum was not a public place that could be made secure like the Congress or the Department of State. When I arrived there was still a group of tourists there. I felt so anxious I couldn't visit the museum galleries after the meeting that had been organized with about fifty other people. I don't know who they were. It was a room with a rostrum, and they used an overhead projector to display the pictures. I spoke only for a few minutes, then left.

'We also met Samantha Power, the former American ambassador to the United Nations, and John McCain, the Republican senator. Samantha Power watched the film that the Syrian National Movement had made. She cried when she saw the images. I like the music in the film, it's gentle but dramatic. Samantha Power said she was sorry that the world could see such atrocities and they couldn't do anything.

'John McCain was very critical about Barack Obama. He told me the president didn't want to meet me. You could tell straight away that this man was very supportive of the Syrian people. He had lots of files on his desk with photos of chemical attacks in Ghouta and others of dead detainees.

'When I walked in, he greeted me warmly. Then he slapped the table with one of the files. He was angry with the American president. "Bashar will do far worse than that if Barack Obama does not draw the line at this policy of violence!" He talked for a quarter of an hour about the regime, the Free Syrian Army, Daesh. I was surprised to see how much he knew about the situation in Syria, as if he lived there himself.

'Then we prepared for the congressional hearing, which was so important in my view. We discussed the best way to address Congress. In a closed or open session? The congressman explained the difference to me. In closed sessions, members of Congress ask questions and you reply, but nothing is released to the press. I was afraid, but I had come to tell the world, to talk about the abuses of the regime. So I had to address an open session. He did everything he could to ensure my safety. That reassured me.

'We entered Congress through a tunnel. One of those wide tunnels like those hotel corridors that link different buildings. Nothing like the tunnels dug by the Free Syrian Army! We arrived in the office of the leader of the House, where we waited a while, maybe fifteen minutes. We drank fruit juice to unwind a bit.

'They told me how the session would pan out. I would sit in the room, in the front row, facing the stage where the members of Congress were sitting. The journalists and photographers would come in through the back door and take photos, which would prove that I had come to bear witness to Congress. But none of the media would be allowed to film me or film the scene face on.

'I was very afraid that the journalists might jeopardize my security and what we had set up in the room. They had would have only ten minutes to take their photos from behind.

'Members of Congress and members of human rights organizations would be sitting facing me. I had been assured that all communications, telephones and cameras that normally record the debates would be cut. Everything went according to plan. Throughout the hearing, I was disguised by my baseball cap, my large sunglasses and my blue hoodie.

'At first, the sound of the flashes and clicks of the cameras by the journalists took me back to the work I used to do for the regime. I sometimes had to use a flash in the morgue at Tishreen hospital, when there wasn't enough light.

'Then the police ushered the journalists out. So now I could look right and left for the first time and see a bit more of the room. Blown-up photos of the dead detainees were on display around the room. Then I realized their value and the importance of what I had done. I felt proud. I remembered when I had taken the photos, I recognized them. Of course, I didn't remember the individuals in detail, but their facial features were etched in my memory. For two years I had done nothing else but take photos and archive them.

'The chair of the House Committee on Foreign Affairs [Ed Royce], who was leading the session, gave everyone a chance to speak.

'In his introduction he welcomed me and acknowledged the value of what I had done. During the session, because I was afraid that my voice would be recognized, I spoke quietly to a translator who then transmitted what I had said at full volume to the members of Congress. I read a text I had prepared, in which I explained my work and how I had left Syria. It was a message to the world. I spoke for about ten minutes. Then I replied to questions and commented on the photos. Even though they spoke for themselves. They didn't really need further explanation.

'Someone tried to argue that the photos had been taken by the opposition. I told him my history, how I had taken them and how the numbers on the bodies worked.

'When the session came to an end, another person dressed like me – with a baseball cap, dark glasses and the same blue hoodie – was ushered out through the door at the front. He was a decoy for the journalists, who had been waiting outside for the last two hours.

During that time, we were in the office of the chair of the House Committee on Foreign Affairs.

'Like John McCain, he poked gentle fun at my baseball cap. "A shame you didn't choose another team", he said. "We might have got along better. You'll have to change it." John McCain had said with a smile: "Why did you choose that team? I don't like them. It's a shame. We could have made sure you didn't wear it." I didn't know anything about these teams. Afterwards, I asked for a cap with nothing written on it!

'Before leaving Congress, we had lunch – hamburgers, of course. Then we left via the tunnel.

'I was pleased I had made sure the voice of Syria was heard. Not everyone was in a position to do that. We stayed about a week in Washington. It's a very beautiful city. I was surprised to see poor people sleeping under a bridge or in tents, quite near to the White House. I had never imagined that there were poor people in a country such as the United States. In Syria we always dream about visiting the European countries and the US. We think of them as heaven on earth. But it turns out that even here there is poverty and class distinctions.

'We went to the White House to see Barack Obama, but he didn't receive us. We were told he was in a conversation with Putin. So we left him a letter. We met one of his advisers. I was shown round the Oval Office. It was nice. I never thought I'd get to see somewhere like this. It's not the person who works there that counts, but rather the way he behaves towards to the world. I would have had a higher opinion of Barack Obama if he had taken responsibility in dealing with Bashar al-Assad.

'When we reached the end of the visit, we sat in a meeting room, where they asked me the same questions the members of Congress had. It was unfortunate that we hadn't met Barack Obama. But the main thing was that we had passed on the message to Congress, that we had delivered the words of the Syrian people, to make the world face up to its human and moral responsibilities concerning what was happening in the detention centres and prisons of Syria.

'When the presidents of the great powers have a real political will, they will put an end to Bashar al-Assad's crimes and change the destiny of tens of thousands of detainees still in prison.

'Am I a hero? Is there something special about me that I went to the office of the president of the United States and met Senator McCain? I'm just like any other Syrian. What is important is the cause I defend. I left Syria to advance the Syrian cause. We still haven't yet gathered the fruits we have sown. After all the dangers we faced, I still don't know if that harvest will come. We have worked hard in the hope of this harvest. So that the regime and all those responsible are brought before justice. That will be the harvest.'

Washington, Capitol Hill

That Thursday, 31 July 2014 at 9.30 a.m., Ed Royce, the chair of the predominantly Republican House Committee on Foreign Affairs, opened a session entitled 'The Assad killing machine exposed: consequences for US policy'. 'Today we, members of the committee, examine the evidence of horrific atrocities committed by the regime of Bashar al-Assad against the Syrian people. ... [T]he Syrian crisis is now in its fourth year – this is a crisis created and sustained by Bashar al-Assad, who responded to peaceful demands ... for their universal rights ... with unspeakable violence, including violence against children ... We are honoured to be joined by ... Caesar, a defector from Syria, who risked his life to smuggle out of Syria over 50,000 photos of political dissidents tortured and killed by the regime after the protest began. I offer you a special thanks for speaking here today before our committee.'[1]

In the room, Caesar sat in the front row, facing Ed Royce. His face was almost completely masked by his cap and the hood of his blue windcheater: only his nose was showing. He was sitting next to Mouaz Moustafa. This former Senate staffer and executive director of the Syrian Emergency Task Force, which supports opposition groups, had been arguing for the arming of the rebels for months. In May 2013, he accompanied John McCain on a secret mission to the north of Syria to meet Salim Idriss, the then commander of the Free Syrian Army.

It was Mouaz Moustafa who had organized Caesar's visit. In Congress, he was the one who translated his speech. Caesar leaned over to him and murmured the words, which he wrote in blue pen on two sheets of paper in his fine handwriting:

'[I]t is a great honor for me to be here in this house of democracy, and I deeply thank you for giving me the chance to come here and speak to you with all honesty, with transparency, and with love.

'I am a Syrian national that has come here to speak to you with the simplicity of Syrian farmers, Syrian farmers that have been marginalized by Bashar al-Assad and by his father before him. I am not a politician, and I don't like politics. And neither am I a lawyer. And, although I have great respect for the law, I don't know much about its details. I am a military man that worked for the military police that was under the guise of the department of defence. ...

---

1 https://foreignaffairs.house.gov/wp-content/uploads/2016/08/7-31-14-briefing.pdf, accessed 19 July 2017.

'And I had the job of taking pictures of any death that had happened within the military establishment in Syria before the Revolution and after the beginning of the Revolution. Our work multiplied greatly during the Revolution. And the bodies of those incarcerated were being sent to the military hospitals of the regime, and we would be called to go there and take photographs of it, depending on the demand. But I did not only have access to the bodies that I took pictures of myself, but I had the access to look at all of the pictures taken by other photographers, as well, because me, along with one colleague, I had the responsibility of downloading the pictures and archiving them on the state computers ...

'I have seen horrendous pictures and bodies of people that had tremendous amounts of torture, like deep wounds and burns and strangulation. And bodies that had their eyes gouged out, as well as bodies that were severely beaten, horrible beatings that ended up in breaking of bones, and horrible bruises on the face and body, and bodies that were emaciated and very skinny. People starved to death, and their bodies looked like skeletons. These people died of starvation.

'I have never in my life seen pictures of bodies that were subjected to such criminality, except when I saw the pictures of the victims of the Nazi regime.

'I saw pictures of the bodies of young children, and the very elderly as well, and pictures of women. And sometimes I would actually run across pictures of some of my own neighbors and some of my friends that I actually recognized. I would be heartbroken for them, but I would not dare tell their own families, and could not even communicate what had happened to their children, because death would have been my fate if the regime found out that I was leaking out regularly secret information.

'My work ethic, my morals, my religion did not allow me to be quiet about these horrendous crimes that I see. And I felt as if I was a partner to the regime in these horrendous crimes that I was taking photos of. I directly decided that I should defect ... And after conversations between me and a trusted source within the Revolution, they advised me that I not defect until I complete my mission of being able to get as many pictures as possible, and as much evidence as possible of these crimes.

'And so, I would regularly give them pictures that I was taking and that I was seeing every day, and took pictures also from the state computers that I had access to, and also from the monthly archive that we had. And then, when I started to become a bit more scared, and I felt that there was imminent danger on my life, I told my contact that it is now important for me to defect and escape, and he helped me in that regard. And he helped provide me with the right conditions to allow me to escape from Syria.

'I have come to your honourable Congress to give you a message from the people of Syria. The first is what is going on in Syria is a genocidal massacre that is being undertaken by the biggest terrorist out there, Bashar al-Assad. He destroyed the country, and he killed his own people with no mercy. And he released the terrorists from his own jails, so they can spread corruption in Syria and outside of Syria.

'And, second of all, these bodies that we have, way more than 10,000 bodies that we have pictures of, no one here can bring their life back to them. But I am here to tell you that there are more than 150,000 people incarcerated still in the jails of Assad. And their fate will be the same fate of those ones that I have taken pictures of.

'The Syrian people are demanding and hoping and wishing that your emotions, your morals, your values would be moved within you. We have known you to be humanitarian people and moral people in the past. You have stopped, with your brave decision-making, deaths that happened in Yugoslavia and other places.

'And I would like to end with the words of God: "He who kills a soul – he who kills an innocent soul only to kill a soul or for corruption in the land, it is as if he has killed the entirety of humanity. And he who saves a single soul, it is as if has saved the entirety of humanity."

'And thank you all very much, and may peace be upon you, and the grace and blessings of God.'[2]

There was complete silence in the room. The enlarged photos of the detainees covered the walls. David Crane, the former prosecutor who had written the first report on the affair back in January 2014, was sitting quite close to Caesar. Imad Eddine al-Rachid savoured the reaction of the thirty or so Representatives present. No one was in any doubt concerning the authenticity of the photos. The Syrian political opponent thought he had gained support through bringing the crimes of the regime to their attention.

Jan Karski, a 1943 Precedent

Seventy-one years earlier, almost to the day, a man came to Washington also to be a witness to crimes against humanity – crimes that would subsequently be labelled genocide. He got to meet the president of the United States: 'The White House seemed to me like a large country estate, brand new and well built ...', Jan Karski wrote in his book. 'I thought about what

---

2 Text available at: https://foreignaffairs.house.gov/wp-content/uploads/2016/08/7-31-14-briefing.pdf, accessed 19 July 2017.

such a building would be in my country. ... My heart beat faster ... I was at the very heart of the citadel of power. I was about to meet the most powerful man in the world.'[3]

Karski was a Pole. He wanted to alert the Allies to the extermination of the Jews by the Nazis. A resistance fighter, he was arrested by the Soviets and handed over to the Germans in a prisoner exchange. He escaped from a train, but was recaptured – by the Gestapo this time – and tortured, before escaping again. In August 1942, he secretly smuggled himself into the Warsaw ghetto and then the Izbica Lubelska concentration camp, not far from Belzec. The leaders of the Jewish community asked him to bear witness to the world on the unfolding genocide. He wrote the famous 'Karski Report' on the Final Solution and the situation in Poland under Nazi occupation.

After passing through London, where he was received by members of the British cabinet, Karski arrived in Washington on 28 July 1943, while war was still raging in Europe. His meeting with Franklin D. Roosevelt lasted an hour and a quarter.

On 28 July 2014, Caesar, the Syrian, was at the Holocaust Museum in Washington. His first public appearance, four days before his testimony before the US Congress. "When we met him, we thought a lot about Karski', says Cameron Hudson, the director of the Center for the Prevention of Genocides at the Holocaust Museum. 'Karski met Roosevelt and obtained nothing that might put an end to the Final Solution.' But the two

---

3 Jan Karski, *Mon Témoignage devant le monde* [My testimony to the World] (Robert Laffont, 2010). An English translation (not used here) has been published as *Story of a Secret State: My Report to the World* (Simon Publications, 2001).

men are very different. Karski was a resister, Caesar has never claimed to be a human rights activist. He became one. He never set out to be a hero, but he is one now. 'We looked at him when he stood in front of us', says Cameron Hudson, 'and we asked ourselves what we would have done in his shoes.'

The inscription at the entrance to the building, 'Never again', recalls the museum's mission. A place of both memory and an advance alert, the museum has exhibitions on the Tutsi genocide and the one in Darfour, the Khmer Rouge massacres between 1975 and 1979 and those in Bosnia between 1992 and 1995.

With Caesar's photos, the museum's director found himself face to face with a present-day drama that represented everything he was fighting against: 'The photos of the bodies, the methods used to kill people, the systematic documentation and archiving, the numbers – all this, of course, is reminiscent of the Holocaust. I don't want to compare, even though this shows a level of organization that you only see in situations of genocide and where there is a concerted political will to eradicate a section of the population.'

Then, clearly shocked, he added: 'What was surprising was that these photos had been taken recently. It's not something that dates from seventy, forty or even twenty years ago. These events were taking place at the time we were looking at and paying attention to the photos. This changes the nature of the discussion. This is not a historical discussion but, rather, a contemporary one. This raises the question of our responsibility. I have no responsibility for what took place in the Holocaust, but I do for what is happening in the world where I live now. That is why we decided to make a selection of the photos and display them in our museum.' Since October, ten or so of the photos had been permanently projected in a gallery at the museum.

The museum was conceived to give citizens such as Karski and Caesar a chance to be heard. But Caesar would not be heard by the American presidency. At the White House, the meeting between the Syrians and the two National Security advisers to vice-president Joe Biden was tense. The normally calm Imad Eddine al-Rachid became heated and reproached them for promising nothing but humanitarian aid: 'Bashar al-Assad's planes bomb us and kill us. We'd rather live with empty bellies than die with full ones. Instead of spending money on food, go and buy something that will stop the planes killing Syrians.' And then he added that the Syrians were beginning to understand that their lives seemed to have no value as far as the United States was concerned.

Caesar left a handwritten letter to Obama: 'I risked my life and exposed my family to extreme danger in order to stop the systematic torture practised by the regime against its prisoners ... What can you do to prevent these murders, especially when there are known to be more than 150,000 prisoners in prisons awaiting their terrible fate?'

Where Is Justice?

Caesar's file embarrassed the American administration, which clearly didn't want to deal with the 'Assad question'. Their priority was air strikes against the jihadists of Islamic State, who were occupying swathes of Iraqi and Syrian territory and, most importantly, were threatening the security of European countries and inciting terrorist attacks. A meeting with the FBI finally convinced Imad Eddine al-Rachid that the Caesar file was an inconvenience. The Syrian had handed over about 27,000 photos of detainees to the FBI. Using their facial recognition software and the huge database in the possession of the federal authorities (photos supplied with visa or passport applications archived in the State Department or photos in the database of terrorists), the FBI had promised to find the Americans or Syro-Americans among the dead detainees. This was an important element in opening legal proceedings in the United States.

'We were very disappointed in the attitude of the FBI', Imad Eddine al-Rachid explains. 'We really thought that they would help us, but as it turned out, we were rather a nuisance to them. They didn't want to reply to our question whether there were any American victims. They made out that some of the photos were technically of poor quality and couldn't be analysed.'

Stephen Rapp, the American ambassador at large in charge of international justice, who was present at this meeting, explains that only 5,500 of the 27,000 photos were usable. 'When we initiated this facial recognition project, I thought we would find a hundred or so matches. We have millions of photos in our databases. But we got only ten matches.' Passing through London in March 2015, he opened up his laptop to show two photos of two men who had a strange resemblance to each other: one dead in a detention centre of the Syrian regime, the other alive on an identity card photo. 'We couldn't be 100 per cent sure it was the same person. We needed further tests.'

This former prosecutor on the International Criminal Tribunal for Rwanda and then on the Special Tribunal for Sierra Leone admitted that he was frustrated by both judicial and political progress. 'When I was working on Rwanda and Sierra Leone, I heard so many terrible witness statements for which there was no corroborating evidence. But Caesar's photos ... I have never seen such clear evidence of war crimes and crimes against humanity.'

One year after Caesar's visit to its offices, the FBI finally announced officially that the photos in the file were genuine. In a five-page report submitted to the State Department in June 2015, a copy of which was obtained by the website Yahoo News, the FBI declared that the photos 'have not been manipulated ... They show real people and events.' There was plenty here to embarrass the American administration as it worked towards its nuclear agreement with Iran, the other principal ally of Bashar al-Assad alongside Russia.

However, the demands of realpolitik meant that a referral to the International Criminal Court was currently impossible. The establishment of ad hoc tribunals, such as those convened for former Yugoslavia and Rwanda, also required the agreement of the UN Security Council, so the Russians and the Chinese needed to be on board.

Even the hybrid tribunals involving national and international magistrates owed their existence to an agreement of the UN: in Sierra Leone, to try the perpetrators of war crimes and crimes against humanity during the armed conflict; in Cambodia, to prosecute the crimes of the Khmer Rouge; in Lebanon, to prosecute, in particular, the perpetrators of the assassination of the former Lebanese prime minister Rafik Hariri on 14 February 2005.

Today, the Caesar file could be part of a new phase of international justice: one where national tribunals might deal with crimes adjudged sufficiently serious to be of concern to the whole international community, crimes of torture, war crimes, crimes against humanity, genocide. Thus France tried and sentenced a Rwandan for complicity in genocide in March 2014 thanks to a mechanism known as 'universal jurisdiction', which allows you to open an inquest against foreign persons on your own territory.

Uncompromising Evidence

In a major European city, which has to remain nameless for reasons of security, one man banks on this ability of national tribunals to apply international justice. The Canadian William Wiley is a former international prosecutor. Along with other international lawyers who had worked on former Yugoslavia, Iraq or Rwanda, he leads the Commission for International Justice and Accountability. Founded in The Hague in 2012 and financed by the European Union, the UK and the US, its aim is to collect evidence of war crimes and crimes against humanity committed in Syria and to prepare key documents for future legal proceedings against their perpetrators.

'National jurisdictions don't have the means to conduct inquests such as this', William Wiley explains. 'They don't have enough money or time and, more than anything, can't take the risks that we can.' In Syria, as the war has gone on, fifty or so individuals have been collecting as many documents on the regime as possible. As soon as a zone, a town, a quarter, a municipal building falls into the hands of rebels of the Free Syrian Army, the evidence hunters gather up every last scrap of written documentation they can lay their hands on. Destination: the headquarters of the CIJA.

In the peaceful confines of their offices, far from the sound of the bombs, they have scanned nearly 500,000 pages of documents. A large proportion of these have been analysed by military and political experts and used to interpret the functioning of the Syrian regime and its chain of command. All the Baath party top officials, the military commanders and the directors of the intelligence services have been identified.

The CIJA's work is methodical, painstaking and relentless. Four files containing the names of twenty-four suspects have been drawn up: three against important members of the regime, one against those of the armed opposition groups. Alongside this, new documents continue to be gathered. In spring 2015, the CIJA agreed to an exchange of data with the lawyers working on the Caesar affair. William Wiley and the international lawyer Toby Cadman would work together on this. Cadman was, at that time, a member of the 9 Bedford Row International chambers in London, which had picked up the baton from Carter-Ruck and Co., the authors of the report commissioned by Qatar.

'We have arrest orders naming hundreds of individuals', says one senior member of the CIJA, who wishes to remain anonymous. 'Activists targeted by the regime for having organized demonstrations, communicated with foreign media or posted videos on the internet.' So many names that the CIJA could cross-reference with the 27,000 photos of dead detainees in the Caesar file, of which the commission had a copy. Irrefutable proof of the death machine.

Defying Fear to Bear Witness

Like William Wiley, Toby Cadman was involved in a race against the clock to gather documents that would prove the systematic policy of torture and murder on the part of the regime. His team had got hold of, among other things, an order of the regime mentioning 'a problem in the detention centres ... which needs to be resolved now'. The order was transmitted in spring 2012, when observers from the United Nations were due to come to Syria to evaluate the situation on the ground. They were due to visit the prisons and detention centres in particular. By cross-referencing this information with other documents, which Toby Cadman prefers to keep confidential for the time being, they were able, according to him, to be almost completely certain that this conjunction of events signified that 'the regime decided to execute en masse a large number of detainees in order to empty out the detention centres and render them more presentable for the duration of the visit'.

For Toby Cadman, the essential thing is to secure the evidence and record witness statements. In London, his chambers want to launch proceedings in countries which have signed up to universal jurisdiction. Spain, Germany, Portugal, Belgium, the UK, Norway, the Netherlands or South Africa, for example, recognize this jurisdiction with only minor restrictions. In early summer 2015, 9 Bedford Row International claimed that it could already open proceedings in Spain and in the UK. It would do so two years later with Guernica 37, the office Cadman founded with the international lawyer Almudena Bernabeu. 'The more we initiate proceedings, the more pressure we put on international community', Toby Cadman suggests. 'This also, and above all, means that we don't have to wait years to record testimonies. All we need is to find the families of victims whose photos appear in the Caesar file and who are willing to file a case.'

This is quite a challenge. Fear is still deep-rooted and the repression in Syria so efficient that Syrians in exile abroad do not dare present themselves before justice if members of their families are still living in Syria in zones under the control of the state. Caesar himself, who lives in constant fear of being recognized, has refused to give testimony in the UK or Spain.

In Istanbul, the family of Khaled, the former works foreman from Daraya who was arrested and whose numbered body was found among Caesar's pictures, agreed to file a case. Some distance away from Syria, they now feel safe. After the bribes they paid to inter-mediaries who lied to them by telling them that Khaled was still alive in one of the cells of Air Force intelligence, justice is the only thing now available to them. To help bring criminals to trial. 'What else can we do?' Ahmed, Khaled's older brother, asks with an awkward smile. 'We are doing all that people like us can do. We don't have any choice. If we don't testify, it is as if we have died a second time. Revolutions are the people's grave.'

In France, the Foreign Ministry, like the FBI before it, has been busy looking for French or Franco-Syrian victims among the dead detainees. In summer 2015, the legal department of the ministry acquired copies of a number of the photos. 'If we find a French citizen we can refer it to the state prosecutor and ensure that a judicial process is launched', a ministry spokesperson says. 'We weren't able to invoke the International Criminal Court, so we are seeking other ways to bring Bashar al-Assad to account.'

In this summer of 2015, Sami and Caesar no longer have faith. The two men were forced to leave their homeland two years earlier, bringing with them to the free world and its justice system a hard drive filled with photos of emaciated, tortured bodies, with numbers written on their skin. Two years on, the Syrian death machine continues its macabre routine. And still so few answers. No one has yet been able to explain and illuminate the significance of the series of numbers on the bodies of the dead detainees. Are the numbers given to the detainees when they enter prison or are they assigned to their dead bodies when they leave?

'We still have no information about how this works in detail because Syrians are afraid to speak', Sami rages bitterly. 'The war has been going on for four years. Diplomats talk about reconciliation and transition. Does that mean the members of intelligence services will still be in place? After all this? And that Caesar and I will still be hunted by the regime …?'

Thousands of kilometres from this city in northern Europe where the two men have sought refuge, Syrian families scrutinize the photos every day, one after another, in the hope of spotting a facial feature, an expression, that will allow them to recognize one of their own. A morbid search on the internet, while in the throes of suffering.

'The international community has abandoned Syria and betrayed the blood spilled', Caesar would write to me later, after the fall of Aleppo in 2016. 'We have knocked on so many doors to expose the crimes of the regime, which show no mercy to anyone. But all these doors were shut in our faces. But what is going on is not just a Syrian concern, not just an Arab or a Muslim concern. It goes much further than that. It is a concern for the whole of humanity.'

Appendix 1

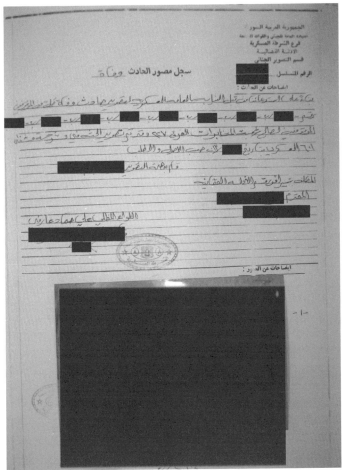

A form from the department of criminal photography of the military police, copied by Caesar.

Appendix 2

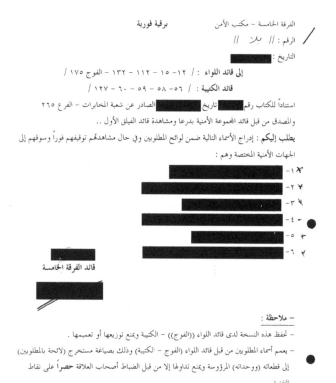

الفرقة الخامسة – مكتب الأمن   برقية فورية

الرقم : // بلا //

التاريخ :

إلى قائد اللواء : / ١٢ – ١٥ – ١١٢ – ١٣٢ – الفوج ١٧٥ /

قائد الكتيبة : / ٥٦ – ٥٨ – ٥٩ – ٦٠ – ١٢٧ /

استناداً للكتاب رقم   تاريخ   الصادر عن شعبة المخابرات – الفرع ٢٦٥

والمصدق من قبل قائد المجموعة الأمنية بدرعا ومشاهدة قائد الفيلق الأول ..

يطلب إليكم : إدراج الأسماء التالية ضمن لوائح المطلوبين وفي حال مشاهدتهم توقيفهم فوراً وسوقهم إلى الجهات الأمنية المختصة وهم :

١-
٢-
٣-
٤-
٥-
٦-

قائد الفرقة الخامسة

– ملاحظة :

– تحفظ هذه النسخة لدى قائد اللواء ((الفوج)) – الكتيبة ويمنع توزيعها أو تعميمها .

– يعمم أسماء المطلوبين من قبل قائد اللواء (الفوج – الكتيبة) وذلك بصياغة مستخرج (لائحة بالمطلوبين) إلى قطعاته (ووحداته) المرؤوسة ويمنع تداولها إلا من قبل الضباط أصحاب العلاقة حصراً على نقاط التفتيش .

Order of arrest issued by the 5th Division. The document was retrieved by the Commission for International Justice and Accountability.

Appendix 3

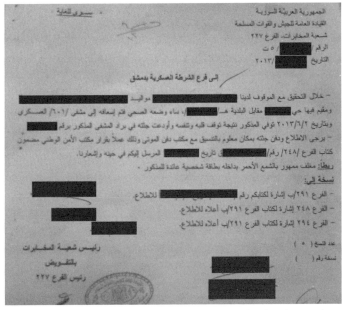

Interment order for a detainee who died of 'cardiac
arrest and respiratory failure' during his interrogation.
Copied by Caesar on his mobile phone.

Appendix 4

The Structure of the Prison in branch 215

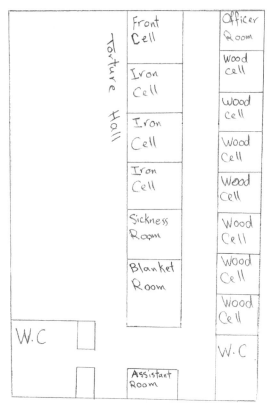

Sketch of the floor of Branch 215 where Ahmad al-Riz was detained.

Appendix 5

Branches of the intelligence services and divisions of the army from which came the dead detainees whose photos appear in the Caesar file. The document was drawn up by the Caesar group.

1 Branch 215 of the military intelligence services (raids)
2 Branch 248 of the military intelligence services (investigation)
3 Branch 227 of the military intelligence services (Al Mantaqa)
4 Branch 235 of the military intelligence services (Palestine)
5 Branch 220 of the military intelligence services (from the Sassa region)
6 Branch 216 of the military intelligence services
7 Branch 291 of the Air Force intelligence services (investigation)
8 Branch 293 of the military intelligence services
9 Branch 261 of the military intelligence services (Homs branch)
10 Branch 295 of State Security

11　Branch 251 of State Security
12　Department of General Intelligence (state safety)
13　Air Force intelligence services (information branch)
14　Air Force intelligence services
15　Republican Guard
16　1st Armoured Division
17　4th Armoured Division
18　9th Armoured Division
19　Border Guard
20　1st Armoured Division, Regiment 141
21　Regiment 274
22　Artillery and rocket administration, Regiment 157
23　Branch of the military police (detective)
24　National Defence, a member of the *shabiha* (pro-government militia)

Appendix 6

Excel spreadsheet established by the Caesar group, showing the characteristics of the detainees photographed.

No	Branch	Young	Minor	Elderly	Total victims	slimness	Skin Injury	Light Torture	Chemical Materials	Gouge out Eyes	Lesions	Tattoo	Choke	Electrocution	Severe Torture	Trace of Whips	Conclusive Wounds	New Blood Trace	Herniated Intestine	Medical Procedure	Break	Splint	Holes in Flesh	Tashahhud	Surgery	Physical Disability	Grand Total
1	215	3170	72	290	3532	1961	702	1182	5	189	158	181	30	0	8	1	6	67	0	24	5	0	4	26	1	2	4552
2	227	1843	33	167	2043	557	456	984	6	180	359	151	32	2	10	1	4	23	1	16	1	1	4	27	4	1	2819
3	216	271	2	20	293	212	210	33	0	54	17	14	15	6	0	1	2	4	0	5	0	2	0	8	2	1	586
4	235	91	0	36	127	63	46	53	0	12	9	4	0	0	0	0	0	2	0	5	0	0	1	1	0	0	196
5	248	43	2	9	54	24	25	21	0	6	5	2	0	0	1	0	0	0	0	0	0	0	0	0	0	0	84
6	220	44	0	6	50	24	22	12	0	4	5	6	0	0	2	0	3	0	1	2	0	0	1	3	0	0	85
7	251	100	1	9	110	16	10	66	14	0	11	4	0	0	1	0	1	1	0	16	0	0	2	3	0	0	145
8	MP	41	0	4	45	22	17	17	0	3	1	0	1	0	0	0	0	0	0	1	0	0	1	1	0	0	64
9	SAFI	318	2	32	352	44	12	256	1	4	9	10	0	0	8	0	14	20	3	20	2	2	7	10	5	0	427
10	Others	65	0	4	69	4	1	47	6	1	2	0	0	0	1	0	15	18	1	7	1	0	0	1	0	0	105
11	Anonymous reference	101	2	8	111	9	9	67	5	2	9	9	0	0	0	0	20	25	0	6	7	0	2	1	4	0	175
	Grand Total	6087	114	585	6786	2936	1510	2738	37	455	585	381	78	8	31	3	65	160	6	102	16	5	22	81	16	3	9238

Acknowledgements

I would like, first and foremost, to thank Caesar for having agreed to spend so much time telling me his story. Sami's trust was invaluable. Imad Eddine al-Rachid and Hassan Shalabi opened their file to me. The survivors of the detention centres, the many witnesses who appear in this book, shared their memories with me, often with great distress. I will never forget these conversations.

This inquiry could not have happened without the help and essential support of Naïm Kossayer. It would never have been completed without Soussen Ben Cheikh, his translations and numerous interviews, his advice and his research. François Burgat got us past a major obstacle in the inquiry.

Helena D'Elia, of the Centre Primo Levi in Paris, which provides assistance to victims of torture and political violence, listened to my doubts and accompanied me along the way.

Ziad Majed went through the text with a fine-tooth comb and helped me to avoid making mistakes.

I have to thank Patrick Angevin, for his discreet but essential presence during these long months. Lune and Lili for their patience and their smiles.

Acknowledgements

Valérie Parlan and Aïcha Arnaout followed the steps of the inquiry with sensitivity.

I thank François Azouvi and Manuel Carcassonne of Editions Stock for agreeing to publish this book. The patience and care of Capucine Ruat in these last few weeks have been precious and reassuring.

And I have a special thought for the person who gave me the gift of believing through to the end.

Finally, I would like to pay homage to Wladimir Glasman, that indefatigable observer of the Syrian crisis, who died on 21 August 2015. His sharp eye helped me to understand the layout of the places of torture and the hospitals where the bodies were photographed.

Select Bibliography

A select bibliography of books and websites that have helped me in the course of this inquiry. For providing context in understanding extermination and concentration camp systems. To learn how to interview my witnesses then transcribe their words in a way that is faithful to their reality. I thank the authors below.

François Burgat and Bruno Paoli (eds), *Pas de printemps pour la Syrie*, La Découverte, 2013

Varlam Chalamov, *Récits de la Kolyma*, Verdier, 2003

Père Patrick Desbois, *Porteur de mémoires*, Michel Lafon, 2007; new edition, Flammarion, collection 'Champs Historie', 2009

Caroline Donati, *L'Exception syrienne. Entre modernisation et résistance*, La Découverte, 2009

Jean-Pierre Filiu, *Je vous écris d'Alep, au cœur de la Syrie en révolution*, Denoël, 2013

Jean Hatzfeld, *Dans le nu de la vie. Récits des marais rwandais*, Le Seuil, 2003

Nicolas Hénin, *Jihad Academy, Nos erreurs face à l'Etat islamique*, Fayard, 2015

Select Bibliography

Jan Karski, *Mon Témoinage devant le monde*, Robert Laffont, 2010; translated as *Story of a Secret State: My Report to the World*, Simon Publications, 2001

Samuel D. Kassow, *Qui écrira notre histoire? Les archives secrètes du ghetto de Varsovie*, Grasset, 2011; new edition, Flammarion, collection 'Champs Histoire', 2013

Mustafa Khalife, *Al-Qawqa'a*, Dar al-Adab, 2008

Hala Kodmani, *La Syrie promise*, Actes Sud, 2014

Primo Levi, *If This Is a Man and The Truce*, Penguin, 1979

Ziad Majed, *Syrie. La Révolution orpheline*, Actes Sud. 2014

Maria Malagardis, *Sur la piste des tueurs rwandais*, Flammarion, 2012

Jean-Pierre Perrin, *La Mort est ma servante. Lettre à un ami assassiné, Syrie (2005–2013)*, Fayard, 2013

Yassin al-Haj Saleh, *Récits d'une Syrie oubliée. Sortir la mémoire des prisons*, Les Prairies ordinaires, 2015

Michel Seurat, *Syrie. L'Etat de barbarie*, PUF, 2012

The Syrian Association for Missing and Conscience Detainees (SAFMCD) has put some photos from Caesar's file online: http://www.safmcd.com

The blog of the former diplomat Wladimir Glasman, a connoisseur of Syria: http://syrie.blog.lemonde.fr/

The Centre Primo Levi, which provides assistance to victims of torture and political violence: http://www.primolevi.org

The websites of human rights organizations, both international and Syrian, which publish regular reports:

Human Rights Watch: http://www.hrw.org/org

Amnesty International: http://www.amnesty.org

Violations Documentation Center: http://www.vdc-sy.
  info/index.php/en/
Syrian Network for Human Rights: http://www.sn4hr.
  org